Teachers, computers and
the classroom

TEACHERS, AND THE

edited by
Ivan Reid and James Rushton

COMPUTERS
CLASSROOM

Manchester University Press

Published by
Manchester University Press
Oxford Road, Manchester M13 9PL, U.K.
51 Washington Street, Dover, N.H. 03820, U.S.A.

British Library cataloguing in publication data
Teachers, computers and the classroom.
  1. Computer-assisted instruction
  I. Reid, Ivan II. Rushton, James
  371.3′9445   LB1028.5

Library of Congress cataloging in publication data
Teachers, computers, and the classroom.
  Includes index.
  1. Computer-assisted instruction—Addresses, essays,
lectures. 2. Education—Curricula—Data processing—
Addresses, essays, lectures. I. Reid, Ivan.
II. Rushton, James.
LB 1028.5.T37 1985   371.3′9445   85-2896
ISBN 0–7190–1774–2

Photoset in Linotron Plantin
by Northern Phototypesetting Co., Bolton
Printed in Great Britain
at the Alden Press, Oxford

Contents

Acknowledgements

Chapter 4 appeared as an article in *Research in Education* No. 32 (1984), and is reproduced here with the permission of its authors and the publisher, Manchester University Press. An earlier version of chapter 12 was produced for the International Geographical Union Commission and published in *Computer-assisted Learning in Geographical Education*, ed. N. J. Graves, Institute of Education, University of London, 1984, pp. 86–106. The author, editors and publisher are grateful to Professor Graves for permission to use material. They are also grateful to LAMSAC, London, for permission to reproduce two diagrams from their 1974 report 'Towards a Computer-based Education Management Information System' in chapter 14.

1. Teachers, computers and the classroom: about this book

JAMES RUSHTON and IVAN REID

On 21 June 1948 Professor Tom Kilburn ran the first stored programme on an experimental computer built by Manchester University. The machine was huge and consisted of a series of metal office storage cabinets full of what would now look to a layman like old-fashioned glass valves and other such cumbersome but nonetheless effective components. They took up the whole space of a fairly large room. Some time later, in 1962 or so, the problem of timetabling the activities of a large secondary school was posed to a researcher in the Department of Electrical Engineering. The task was so complex, subtle and unique to the individual school that it was felt to be an uneconomic use of the time of Mercury, the computer and wasteful of the programmer's time.

Compare these anecdotal facts with the state of development today, when it is envisaged, that all schools should possess or have access to a computer of some kind. The development of hardware has been so rapid that in less than forty years some 14 per cent of all households in the UK have a micro computer and most of the users are below the age of twenty-five. Many of them are children of school age. This indeed is rapid progress, by any standard, and it is due in large measure to the development of microcomputers, which put at the disposal of the population at large facilities which were available only to an elite of engineers and researchers thirty-five years ago.

The challenge of the computer to society is more than upon us in the mid-eighties; it has already severely affected some parts of our lives. It has the potential at hand to change quite fundamentally a large number of aspects of social life, from production, administration and commerce to personal shopping and leisure. Further, there appears to be a relentlessness about computer-assisted change, making it difficult to challenge, let alone resist. The entry of this new technology into schools and education has been uncharacteristically swift, owing to government action in supplying machines and providing some impetus. The latter was clearly undertaken by the publication in 1981 of the government-sponsored Micro-electronics Education Programme (MEP), *The Strategy*, and the subsequent work of that organisation. The stated aim was to help schools prepare children for a society in which the use of micro-electronics was commonplace. Unusually for a government document, the report provides useful details of how schools, teachers and children could be prepared for this 'new' world. At the same time government policy and money have quickly led to the physical presence of one or more microcomputers in nearly every school.

The arrival of hardware has preceded the education of teachers to cope with it. While efforts in pre- and in-service education to rectify the situation are in hand, this mismatch will continue for some time. Beyond it is a more fundamental problem. It is not so much the technical snags and lack of knowledge surrounding the use of mircrocomputers as their pedagogic implications that are of concern to schoolteachers. Teachers are appropriately concered with what will happen to their classrooms, their role and their children's learning when the computer and computer-assisted learning (CAL) are commonplace in schools. These concerns are over and probably above those about their ability to cope with the change and challenge of the computer. These implications and concerns tend to be neglected in education for teaching and in the research and literature surrounding the use of computers in schools. Such facts have led to a situation in which many teachers are seeking information on the use of computers in classroom teaching and learning in which the potential of such use is explored, providing a basis for consideration together with models to inform their own practice, whether actual or anticipated. This book sets out to fill this gap in the literature with classroom-based studies and evaluations of computer use.

Many people still think simplistically of computers as taking a lot of drudgery and tedium out of routine tasks. They can achieve such ends with little effort on the part of programmers and users. More imaginative approaches and uses require the human element in the partnership to be more skilful and creative. The imaginative use of computers will, as can be seen in some of the following chapters, lead to enhanced and very subtle teacher-learner interactive situations in classrooms.

All the chapters in the book relate to observation of the use of computers and computer-assisted learning by teachers in their classrooms. As such they offer insights into the 'chalk-face' reality of what many see as a major educational and social innovation. While the contexts of these observations vary, they all deal with a number of common issues and concerns. Chapter 15 identifies and discusses these in the light of the preceding chapters – such questions as, for example, the potential for control of teaching and learning; whether the computer is aid or replacement for the teacher; who is, and will be, the classroom users of computers; what they will be used for; what are the constraints on their use, and what should be the curriculum priorities and strategies for coping with the 'computer age'. It also addresses some of the fundamental considerations underlying the whole enterprise of computers in schools and education in general. They range from the distribution and use of resources, through the equality of access to learning, to the nature and desirability of educational outcomes.

The intervening chapters can be characterised as covering consideration of some theoretical questions, empirical investigation, of computer use and CAL implementation, the evaluation of software and the pragmatic implications of the use of computers and CAL in particular areas of the curriculum. Such a characterisation is, however, misleading to the extent that it suggests a compartmentalisation which does not exist. Readers will find much of interest and utility in all the chapters, including those whose titles may not immediately appear to identify with their specific concerns. The normal teacher signposts of type of school/age of children and curriculum discipline do not apply in that the pedagogic implications of the use of computers and CAL appear generic, as do many aspects of teaching, learning and the classroom. So, for example, while certain chapters (3, 8, 11 and 13) are set in primary schools, and others contextualised within the secondary curriculum (7, 9 and 12), these, like the remaining ones, will be of value to those involved in, or contemplating involvement in, the central concern of this book. There are, then, several ways in which the contents of this book might have been presented and ways in which it might be used. Hopefully the layout described here will allow readers to explore the contents, both using and developing their own initial interests.

Chapters 2 and 3 explore something of the nature of teaching and learning on the one hand, and the implications for them of introducing CAL, on the other. While both raise theoretical issues they do so within the context and light of empirical work in the field. The first of these two chapters maps out in detail the functions of computers, to assess where they can contribute to the teaching-learning process. Its conclusion recognises schooling as a social process and contains the hope that CAL will help to 'reconceptualise the role of teacher' from that of 'industrial foreman' to 'adult guide to the young'. Within the setting of primary schools chapter 3 poses the question of whether the computer is teacher or tool. It argues that there are more exciting things do with micros in the classroom than drill and practice activities. With reference to specific programmes it shows that computers can be used to heighten the cognitive demand of lessons, requiring emphasis on thinking rather than facts and solutions – a challenge for teacher and taught.

Chapters 4 and 5 report empirical investigation of the use of computers and the implementation of CAL in secondary upper schools. Chapter 4 illustrates the 'extent to which schools in the sample are adequately preparing pupils for a perceived society in which computers are commonplace and pervasive', and concludes that only 33 per cent give anything like adequate preparation and that some 50 per cent of school-leavers have had no meaningful interaction with computers. It also highlights some of the school characteristics associated with hardware provision and its use, according to a set of categories of activity. Chapter 5 deals with the teachers' assessment of the extent and context of CAL use in the same schools. Only 13 per cent of the teachers were using CAL, and there was greater use among male and science teachers. The chapter outlines the MEP initiative and lines of resistance to the adoption of CAL. Among its conlusions is that there is little evidence of the development of the new topics listed by MEP, which is itself viewed by teachers as a relatively unimportant source of information. These two chapters demonstrate just how far there is to go in realistically meeting the challenge of the computer in the classroom and in education. They identify many of the problems which will have to be faced and overcome in the near future by the majority of schools and teachers.

Chapter 6 realistically tackles the important question of how teachers can evaluate the usefulness of software (programs) for their classroom teaching. This is clearly a pressing and significant problem.

The chapter contains a detailed schema for evaluation, developed from Reay's work with teachers in the field, both in the UK and in the USA. The check list covers the technical aspects of software and, most importantly, the professional considerations involved in decisions over suitability. Its value lies in the opportunity it provides for the evaluation of software independent of publishers' statements or sales talk or the teachers' 'grapevine'.

Chapters 7–12 look at CAL and computer use in the context of particular parts of the school curriculum – science, language development, physics, mathematics, history and geography – though, as suggested above, their considerations and implications are broad and general. A careful analysis of science lessons in chapter 7 identifies the impact of CAL on learning. The results suggest that it helps to improve qualitatively the learning environment on a number of dimensions by comparison with traditional lessons, though the need to establish the significance of the changes is recognised. The observed changes have importance well beyond the confines of science classrooms. The proportion of more individual and group work, discussion, vocalisation, depth and open-ended questioning and pupil hypothesising will be recognised by most teachers as desirable in themselves, wherever and however they are achieved.

Chapter 8 returns to the primary school classroom, in which Moss has observed the use of adventure game and simulation programs as aids to language development. It includes an analysis of lesson transcripts according to the eleven skills and uses identified for the early years of education by the DES publication *A Language for Life* (the Bullock Report, 1975). The chapter illustrates a useful lesson analysis system which isolates the ways in which objectives of teaching and learning are realised in classroom activity.

Chapters 9 and 10 review studies of the use of the microcomputer, its implications and teachers' reactions in physics and mathematics. To many, these two subjects lie foremost in the implementation of CAL, and appear to be fertile ground. However, chapter 9 concludes, 'even in the hands of electronics enthusiasts we are not going to see physics classes based in a room full of computers carrying out simulated experiments and other forms of second-hand science'. Staff 'are highly critical both of software and poor teaching methods'. Objective tests are called for to confirm the effectiveness of computer use. Chapter 10 contrasts the promise of computers for mathematics – as illustrated in *Mathematics Counts* (the Cockcroft Report, 1982) – and the attendant demands on mathematics teachers, with the availability of staff and teacher education and the views of student and practising teachers. Both chapters (see also chapter 5) emphasise that the responsibilty for implementing CAL and computer studies in schools tends to fall on science and mathematics departments which are traditionally short of staff and under stress. The implications of such findings are clear. Progress towards greater computer and CAL usage in schools is dependent upon the involvement of a broad as possible spectrum of teachers, together with enhanced hardware provision and the development of more suitable and user-friendly software.

Perhaps in some contrast, chapter 11 is concerned with the use of computers in history – not a subject immediately associated with their use. It provides an interesting contrast between the questions asked in similar lessons with and without a computer to answer them and suggests the possibly powerful motivating effect of the computer on research and learning. Again it illustrates the computer's potential not only to assist learning but to improve its quality and to expand its range. Finally, in this area, chapter 12 views some representative lessons in geography involving the use of computer programs. It provides a description, evaluation and illustration of the lessons, which remained strongly teacher-directed. It discusses the reasons for this in terms of the programs used – in this case simulations. Different types of program (as other chapters show) affect the balance of control and initiative in the classroom.

Chapters 13 and 14 explore the development of computer uses which would help teachers in tackling problems with children's creativity and the presentation of written work, and the chore of record-keeping and assessment. A major commerical application of the computer is in word processing, and chapter 13 reports a study of classroom use, including illustrations of children's work. It argues that not only is such experience a useful life/job skill but also/and importantly, that it is potentially a valuable tool for aiding the development of creativity. Research indicates that, to facilitate this, teachers will have to devise means of encouraging pupils to see text revision in terms other than the correction of errors. Chapter 14 demonstrates how effective computers can be in keeping and storing pupils' records and assessments. It discusses the sensitive nature of such operations and the need for close control over them. Records may also be used for devising groupings to facilitate the teaching-learning process.

Unlike much of the wealth of literature to hand about the use of computers in education, this book does not assume that the reader is technically competent in, or familiar with, their use. Nor does it set out to assist readers to that stage. Rather it is addressed to the unsophiscated but interested, and its aim is to inform readers of some of the on-going developments, potential and implications of the classroom use of computers and CAL. It contains a wealth of classroom based information covering a wide spectrum of activities. Clearly it can be neither all-embracing nor pre-emptive. Hopefully, however, it will assist teachers, pupils and others in their interaction with the rapidly developing use of computers in the worlds of learning and life.

2. CAL in the teaching-learning process

P. M. BRADSHAW

Computers, classrooms and clergy

The evaluation of computer-assisted [1]learning presents a number of problems which are exercising the imagination of teachers, but establishing criteria by which to make judgements about the usefulness of computers is an obvious first hurdle. There are two, quite separate areas of uncertainly, the 'functional' and the 'structural'.

The 'functional' problem may be formulated with the question 'What can the computer do to assist learning?' The 'structural' problem can be approached with the question 'Does the advent of the computer give grounds for changing our conceptions of the process of "teaching and learning"?' Attempting to answer the first question is difficult enough – and is the subject of this chapter – but the second is so fundamental that it must be addressed before moving any further. It is a problem which concerns our most elementary assumptions about the nature of knowledge, how it is acquired, and what it is to 'have knowledge'. We can achieve some perspective by comparing the period of change which saw the emergence of printed books with the present.

The impact upon the individual and society of the development of a literate culture is difficult for us to appreciate. The printed book changed our culture fundamentally. We now view the medieval clergy as seeking to maintain a supremacy in matters of 'truth' and how it is 'given' despite the reality of independent and critical thinking made possible by books. Immersed now in that culture, we do not see the waters we swim in. But the emergence of 'informatics', the electronic gathering, processing, storing and transmitting of information, threatens to leave us gasping on beaches we can only begin to imagine.

We, as the champions of the 'new liberalism', are the heirs to that clergy as well as its victors. As teachers of universal literacy we may find our authority as the true source of worthwhile knowledge challenged by CAL. Nor is it enough to claim that the study of a subject still needs the interpretive voice of the 'master', that the learner still needs to be inducted in the dialectic of the subject, the community of interactive minds and voices. The interactive computer is with us now; it is crude, as yet, but developing quickly.

Even more radical and threatening is the emergence of computer-literate young who learn what they know *outside* the classroom and already chafe at the formal guided tour of 'Computer Studies'. Young medieval scholars with a passion for books could own one only at great cost: the young today not only have easy access to computer programs, but also to inexpensive hardware, so that they have the equivalent of the printing press in their own rooms. The medieval reader had to wait upon the supply of books: the modern computer user can create his own library.

Faced with the new, like the medieval clergy, we may consider the idea of computer-based learning as heretical, fantastic or a 'fundamentally mistaken' view of what knowledge is and what is 'worthwhile'. But simply to deny its existence is not an option. It is wiser to acknowledge that the questions one can ask and answer about the computer in the school curriculum have a distinctly provisional and interim character.

For the moment let us address the 'functional' issue: what might teachers expect computers to be able to do to assist pupils to learn?

Computer functions

There are many teachers who are using CAL imaginatively and successfully. As always, there will be individuals who, given new tools, will feel their way towards 'good practice'. But such intuitive teachers often find it difficult to explain their practice to others, and traditional diffusion channels are inadequately slow. Meanwhile, for most teachers, the presence of the computer remains a puzzle. Computers are sometimes being used to provide 'light relief' to the serious business of teaching and learning. Sometimes they are seen as a useful alternative means of keeping the dull and the disruptive occupied. When the motivations and excitement generated by the 'new' have faded, the reckoning comes. Both kinds of teacher – the imaginative and the puzzled – are faced with formulating a rationale in answer to the question 'What can the computer do to assist learning?'

How are we to describe where the computer fits in the teaching-learning process when the process itself is so poorly understood? The history of theoretical models of what 'good teaching' is, or might be, is a cautionary tale: the amount of effective teaching based on academic argument is probably insignificant. Intuition, based on practical experience, is the most trusted source of 'truth' about how to teach. Theories seem to provide practical principles of teaching in inverse proportion to their academic rigour and comprehensiveness. Nevertheless, there have been efforts to bridge theory and practice and it is to these that we turn for help.

Bruner (1973) offers a useful starting point:

> . . . the mature organism seems to have gone through a process of elaborating three systems of skills that correspond to the three major tool systems to which he must link himself for full expression of his capacities – tools for the hand, tools for the distance receptors, and tools for the process of reflection.

> Man's use of mind is dependent upon his ability to develop and use tools or instruments or technologies that make it possible for him to express and amplify his powers.

His view that knowledge should be interpreted in terms of the individual's mastery of tools suggests a framework broad enough to encompass the fifteenth-century monk at his desk and the twentieth-century learner at a computer keyboard.

What is central to the thesis is that (a) man is distinctive in his capacity for inventing tools to augment his existing powers; and (b) education is a process of acquisition of mastery of those tools. To be 'educated' is to have been inducted in the mastery of these tools: 'We depend for survival on the inheritance of acquired characteristics from the culture pool rather than from the gene pool. Culture then becomes the chief instrument for guaranteeing survival, with its techniques of transmission being of the highest order of importance' (id., 1967).

The 'printed book' is an immensely powerful tool for the transmission of culture. The computer, in turn, is yet another 'tool'. What makes it especially powerful is its integration of the 'tool functions' as defined by Bruner. The computer can behave as an extension of the user's own powers of reflection and can allow the user to interact with 'tools for the hand', 'tools for the distance receptors'. This interactive relationship between the user and the computer is highly significant for anyone seeking to estimate the latter's contribution to teaching and learning.

It is this integrative power which is explored by Kemmis *et al.* (1977). In their efforts to evaluate early examples of CAL they conclude that (*a*) the assessment of learner performance by prescribed criteria of achievement, in the tradition of the behaviourist model of learning, is inadequate: 'The view of knowledge compatible with the behaviourist position conflates knowledge and information' (1977: 216); (*b*) we need a model of learning which acknowledges the importance of the knowledge which the individual brings to the learning experience; and (*c*) such a model must also acknowledge that knowledge resides not in the ability to recall items of information but in the *acts* of using such knowledge.

> . . . the successful attainment of knowledge . . . is not merely mastery of propositional knowledge about the subject matter domain, it is appropriate usage. The teacher will judge the student to have learned when he speaks of the object in ways which the teacher regards as appropriate. [1977: 208]

> In this view knowledge inheres in action and is revealed by it; it does not precede action. [*Ibid.*, 224]

The process of teaching and learning is dense with activities – behavioural and psychological. Any attempt to 'unpack' the simultaneity of the process into logically distinct features leads to a linearity and simplicity which is fictional. Nevertheless, only in this way can we begin to discern within the process a number of functions which the computer can fulfil.

The model indicates phases of the learning process and their content:

Phase 1	Phase 2	Phase 3	Phase 4	Phase 5
Input	*Access*	*Processing*	*Production*	*Output*
Form	Mode	Operations	Mode	Form
Phenomena	Equipment	Equipment	Equipment	
	Procedures	Procedures	Procedures	

Form: culturally determined ways of representing meaning, feeling and purpose, e.g. a novel, a graph, a bridge.

Phenomena: naturally occurring objects and events, e.g. rocks, rivers, snow, apples and alligators.

Mode: sensory and symbolic means by which the individual receives and transmits information, e.g. listening, observing, reading, manipulating and acting.

Equipment: tools for assisting the individual in the process of getting access to information, solving problems of understanding and representing understanding, e.g. a telescope, a calculator, a typewriter.

Procedures: methods, techniques which the individual employs in order to get access to information, solve problems of understanding and represent that understanding.

Operations: acts of cognition by which the individual solves problems of access to information, understanding and the representation of that understanding.

Such an analysis allows us to conceptualise discrete elements. We can subsequently characterise the actions of a teacher by assigning to him those elements which he can manipulate, and thereby determine, to some extent, the content and experience of learning. These *interventions* constitute the acts of teaching.

The 'closed classroom' or 'classic' teaching style shows the fullest intervention. In such a teaching style a teacher would:

1. Select the subject, topic and the form of that content at the Input phase.
2. Select or determine the mode of access, which equipment is to be used, what procedures are to be learned and/or applied.
3. Set the problems to be solved, the questions to be asked of the content,
4. Select or determine the mode of production of the answer, the equipment to be used and the procedures to be adopted,
5. Determine what form the answer to the problem or question is to take,
6. Select the criteria to be met by the answer(s) to the task.

An 'open classroom' teaching style allows learner choice or initiative at many of the phases. In a very 'open' style the teacher might simply make information available in a variety of forms and expect the learners to formulate their own problems, select or discover the means of access and production, arrive at their own answers and apply their own criteria of success to the product.

The 'computer as tutor' argument proposes that the computer takes over the interventionist role of the teacher to some degree. If teaching styles can be said to lie along a continuum showing varying amounts of intervention, then the Computer Assisted Instruction type of CAL ('Drill and practice') lies at the 'closed teaching' pole. All the initiatives lie with the computer: the learner is guided closely along carefully defined paths towards predetermined goals. The Input form and its content, the Access and Production modes, equipment and most procedures, the Processing problems, equipment, procedures, the Output form and assessment criteria – all are determined by the computer.

Other forms of CAL share the role of the teacher. For example, a teacher might control everything but the final assessment of the Output, which he gives to the computer. Or he might control the Processing phase by determining what tasks the learner is to perform on the data retrieved with the help of the computer. The 'openness' or 'closedness' of a teaching-learning event, then, is the product of a negotiated relationship between the teacher and the computer.

The 'conjectural paradigm' proposed by Kemmis *et al.* (1977) describes a program which lies near the 'open' end of the continuum where the tasks of Processing are not prescribed and devergent thinking is expected and encouraged. The *Mary Rose* is a good example of a program which is relatively open but which the teacher could 'close down' by directing learners to particular procedures, particular questions and so on.

The two variables of teaching style and variety of computer program design make the description and classification of CAL difficult. A CAL program may be designed to be 'open' or 'closed' in style, but the teacher can alter the learning process by his own interventions.

Using the descriptive framework proposed above, we can begin to map out functions of the computer in order to see where it can contribute in the teaching-learning process. By adopting an analytical description we can tease out the choices which are available to the teacher both as computer buyer and as user.

Phase 1. Input

Form

There is nothing new in the forms of representation which the computer makes available. A video recording can present moving images, a film or slide projector can provide excellent-quality images unmatched by a VDU, a textbook can supply text, number and graphics. What is distinctive and new is the integrated nature of the forms of information provided by the computer. Given sophisticated peripherals and more powerful means of storing data and getting access to data stores such as they provided by laser-read discs, a learner could be presented with information which integrates moving and still images, sound, spoken language, text and number in a way which, potentially, makes the current range of audio-visual aids redundant.

CAL function No. 1: a single source of multi-form information.

In terms of 'content' Input within a program, present technology is limited. With the development of 'expert systems' programming and data storage technology, the computer promises access to extensive bodies of information.

Phase 2. Access

Mode

Given the computer's ability to make multi-form data available, it follows that at the phase of Access the same integrative character obtains: the learner may listen, read, observe and manipulate while using a computer. The manipulation of the keyboard and other peripherals (including, soon, voice command) gives a distinctively new dimension to the learner's relationship with external sources of data. The passive character of traditional modes of 'transmission' and 'receiving' information is modified by the learner's active participation, his interactivity with the source of information.

CAL function No. 2: a user-commanded, multi-mode access to data stores.

Equipment

(1) With appropriate peripherals a computer can monitor and record the 'natural world' with unparalleled speed, precision and persistence, making it an extremely powerful 'research instrument'.

CAL function No. 3: a sophisticated research instrument for monitoring natural phenomena.

(2) With other peripherals, the computer gives access to published data which were formerly too numerous to manipulate or too distant to consult. Adams and Jones (1983) describe an convincing example of history students using census data from the nineteeth century.

CAL function No. 4: a means of access to extensive, distant data-stores.

Procedures

As a corollary to the availability of sophisticated means of access to both physical phenomena and data stores, the learner is obliged to master a range of procedural skills which are new and sometimes demanding. That children should be taught how to use a library has been justified in terms of an extended concept of 'literacy'. Similar arguments have been advanced for including 'mediacy' skills (Maddison, 1983; Rowntree, 1982).

CAL function No. 5: inducts learners in procedural knowledge for getting access to data, with subsequent benefits for skills of independent enquiry and learning.

Phase 3. Processing

Operations

The computer imitates human cognition in a number of important respects. Among efforts to explain its significance, the concept of 'inauthentic labour' (Kemmis *et al.*, 1977) is the most powerful. Within any learning task there may be activities which present no problem but the repeated application of familiar operations; this labour is 'inauthentic' in that it is time-consuming, tedious and merely preparatory to the true or authentic labour of problem-solving. Numerical computation is the most obvious example, but there are others. With the help of the following simple model of cognition we can identify significant parallels between human and computer operations and explore the concept of 'authentic' and 'inauthentic' labour further.

1. Investigative operations
   (*a*) Recall
   (*b*) Search
2. Formulative operations
   (*c*) Covergent construction
       (i) Deduction
       (ii) Reconstruction
       (iii) Application
   (*d*) Divergent construction
3. Evaluative operations
   (*e*) Assessment
   (*f*) Reflection

1. Investigative operations

(a) Recall
The retrieval of information from store. If the learner knows the correct procedures, then clearly the computer is an adjunct to human memory of immense significance.

CAL function No. 6: as an 'aide-mémoire', for quick and errorless recall of data from internal store.

(b) Search
The scanning of a structure (form or phenomenon) in search of particular items of information. Once again, if the learner is master of the procedures, this crucial function can be exploited.

CAL function No. 7: maintains constant, accurate search routines and accumulates record of data found.

2. Formulative operations

(a) Convergent construction
(i) Deduction
The ability of the computer to compute numbers and construct proposition from given rules and data is its most obvious achievement. Together with the 'recall' function, this capacity allows

records of scores to be kept, calculations to be performed without fuss.

CAL function No. 8: solves computational problems quickly and without error.

(ii) Reconstruction

The speed and precision with which the computer 'reconstitutes' a given construct, whether image or text, are famous. The recall or search for information is a constant feature of problem-solving; this repetitive activity is preparatory in much the same way as a great deal of computation is. The computer provides rapid access to information – such as a screen showing a diagram, a map or a list – saving the learner the inauthentic labour of finding and searching through papers. This function is particularly notable when using business packages or playing computer-moderated games, but is valuable whenever the learner needs to consult component content of a subject quickly and repeatedly.

CAL function No. 9: retrieves and represents whole constructs on command.

(iii) Application

The application of rules by which constructs may be manipulated, transformed and reconstructed is errorless and astonishingly fast. Those CAL programs where the learner is invited to make predictions about the effect of changing certain variables – exemplifying the Revelatory paradigm – present, perhaps, the most powerful learning experience. To be able to see what would happen in simulation is rarely possible outside the bounds of CAL.

CAL function No. 10: manipulates and transforms structures, on command, to reveal the complete set of inferences for any given structure.

(b) Divergent construction

Its capacity to generate or calculate all the logical possibilities of a given structure is the nearest the computer comes to imitating human creativity. It can reveal the inferences during a random substitution of variables with a thoroughness and persistence that individuals cannot match. Whether truly creative or not, such a capacity can be valuable to the human operator. As Adams and Jones (1983) suggest, the computer may be used like a kaleidoscope – a machine for the random generation of pleasing structures or 'ideas' which the human inventor can subsequently evaluate and use to fit his own purposes.

CAL function No. 11: generates structures randomly and, by serendipity, creates ideas which interest and satisfy the operator.

3. Evaluative operations

(a) Assessment

'The computer as assessor' is probably its most widely known function. Given that correct responses to tasks can be specified, objective answer tests can easily be programmed. The problems of constructing such tests remain, but the labour of monitoring and calculating is removed.

CAL function No. 12: offers the facility of administering and processing objective answer tests.

Formative assessment probably outweighs summative assessment in its impact upon the learner's progress. The conscientious teacher seeks to induct learners in the habit of checking the quality of the Procedures or methods applied at the Access, Processing and Production phases of the learning process. By providing instruction and evaluative feedback the teacher acts as 'master practitioner' and model; the learners eventually become self-assessing, 'self-disciplined' in the subject. This aspect of teaching is acknowledged to be one of the most important and burdensome, but attending to the simultaneous progress of a classroomful of learners is an almost impossible task. The computer is the ideal answer to the problem. Not only does each child get attention, but the feedback is almost instantaneous.

CAL function No. 13: offers constant, errorless and tireless feedback to the learner engaged in problem-solving.

(b) Reflection

Two cognitive functions which the computer does not imitate are rote learning and reflection. There is no 'rehearsal' in the computer except in terms of recurrent electrical activity. In the case of 'Reflection', because the computer does not match human consciousness, it does not subject ideas to 'critical scrutiny' except in the most limited, codified way.

The whole of this section of the model concerning cognitive operations poses the question 'Whose cognition should the computer imitate, extend and complement – the teacher's or the learner's?'

The use of pocket calculators by schoolchildren is viewed with suspicion by those who believe that it deprives learners of important part of the discipline of mathematics. The computer may emancipate pupils from the drudgery of learning, it is argued, but it also impoverishes the experience of learning. Should children be forbidden to use the computer as a memory store? Is learning by heart an important skill, not to be neglected? Certainly it would be odd to imagine someone claiming to be familiar with English literature who could not recite a single poem. But should children be allowed to use the computer to sort a list of names alphabetically? To construct graphs rather than labour at it themselves? The answer turns upon the answer to another question, 'What kinds of knowledge are worth while?' Perhaps disciplines which require mastery of a large number of procedural skills – of analysis, calculation and conventional representation – benefit from access to a computer. The user of a calculator is no less knowledgeable about what calculation is, conceptually. The person who employs a computer to design and print out a graph is no less knowledgeable about what graphs are, conceptually. To use the computer effectively the learner must –literally – know what he is doing. The fact that what is being done is being done with a tool does not affect the issue of whether the learner knows what he is doing.

To be sure, the skills needed will be different and perhaps *more* demanding than the old ones.

> CAL may extend a teacher's options by embodying in its processes of interaction some of the dynamics and the complexities of higher level learnings. CAL packages are objects for interaction, not merely representations of knowledge; they invite student action and thought . . . [Kemmis *et al.* (1977]

It is not the case that the 'old' tools are being replaced: they are being complemented in a way which makes the processes of understanding salient.

CAL function No. 14: inducts learners in explicit knowledge of how to access, process and represent information.

Papert's thesis (1981) is the fullest expression of this view. A learner engaged in programming, whether in Logo or not, is obliged to reflect upon the nature of cognitive operations. The learner who seeks to construct a computer program about X comes to understand X by acts of Investigation, Formulation and Evaluation. More important, Papert would argue, he or she learns something about the nature of knowledge, something about the nature of constructive ordering which constitutes meaning.

... children are the active builders of their own intellectual structures.

We can learn more, and more quickly, by taking conscious control of the learning process, articulating and analysing our behaviour.

I see the computer as helping in two ways. First the computer allows, or obliges, the child to externalise intuitive expectations. When the intuition is translated into a program it becomes more obtrusive and more accessible to reflection. Second, computational ideas can be taken up as material for the work of remodelling intuitive knowledge. [1981]

CAL function No. 15: provides the opportunity for learners to achieve insight into the nature of the process of the construction of knowledge.

If we examine the computer's contribution to the teacher's tasks we find that the issue of 'computer as teacher' is complicated by uncertainties about what that role is precisely, and by uncertainties concerning the powers of the computer.

The extent to which a computer can act as surrogate teacher is determined, in part, by the level of 'intelligence' of its Processing operations. Important similarities to human cognition have been hypothesised. What the computer cannot be programmed to do (yet) is Reflect upon the quality of the answers the learner may give; that is, 'think about thinking' – which Papert believes to be so important. It can assess correct thinking only in so far as it can match learners' answers against predicted ones. At present, formulating the predicted answers involves a degree of codification which simplifies 'knowledgeable responses' and so ignores answers that are wrong but 'on the right track'. In short, while the computer can measure, it cannot make judgements. In this matter we have made little progress beyond the Programmed Learning tradition. The way ahead to interactive CAL is blocked by the need to 'map out' such responses against an adequate model of the structure of a subject and the teaching interventions necessary to bring about insight. Rushby *et al.* (1981) suggest in their review of CAL that:

The entry of computer assistance or management into the interactions of learning enables more and more complex activities to take place in teaching and so the quality of the experience is heightened. Rarely in Europe did we find agreement or understanding with this approach to education evaluation. As one might expect ... the educational justification for most C.B.L. systems was supplied from a psychometric evaluation model which employed quantitative measures of student performance gain . . . .

Hartley (1981) summarises the position neatly. He suggests that we need:

> . . . a representation of the teaching task so that the programs themselves can compose problems and undertake their solution. When programs have this capacity, the student is able to constuct his own methods and have them analysed by the program.

What can be pursued with more confidence is the production of programs which set questions or tasks for the learner. The skilled teacher will know intuitively what are 'significant problems' in a discipline, even if he cannot say, precisely, what would count as 'knowledgeable responses'. The computer, then can be programmed to set tasks. The evaluative, judgement role of teaching remains beyond current technology.

CAL function No. 16: provides appropriate tasks or questions which lead the learner to understanding.

Phase 4. Production

Mode, procedures

Educational technology already offers the student a wide range of modes, beyond text and number, for representing his understanding. Critics of multi-media approaches to learning point out the heavy demands they make upon material resources and their apparently extravagant use of time and space, compared with traditional modes of representation. The same argument can be deployed against the use of the computer. Literacy is seen as the proper channel for the expression of knowledge: the traditional essay, the writing up of experiments, the whole public examination system give primacy to this mode of representation. The advent of the computer, however, brings fresh impetus to the debate. The number and variety of 'utility programs' available continue to increase, providing learners with an unprecedented array of devices and procedures for the graphical representation of information and ideas.

CAL function No. 17: inducts learners in the mastery of procedures and equipment which improve skills of mediacy.

Equipment

The word-processing facility together with equivalent programs for mathematics are, perhaps, the most significant. But all 'design facilities' are powerful tools for learning, offering the operator the unique opportunity to design, review and revise whole and component problems of calculation, organisation and construction. Revealing the componentiality of design problems, as in the case of Logo programming, alerts the learner to the fundamental elements of the construction of knowledge and its expression

> . . . structures unfold in action. Cognitive structure is manifest in the form of action. Cognitive structures are thus to be found in the structures of action. [Kemmis *et al.* (1977)]

CAL function No. 18: provides devices which augment and extend learners' capacity to design, review and revise their progress towards the production of a final or best draft of a solution.

Phase 5. Output

Form

Very shortly a teacher will find himself presented with a student's history essay which has been prepared with the help of a word-processor and printer. What assessment is appropriate? What criteria should be applied? What does he do about comparing a hand-written essay with one that has had benefit of a high-quality printer? Let us compound the problem: what if the student also has the help of a 'spelling checker' ROM in his computer? These challenges to traditional assessment criteria, of course, are not limited to textual products. They apply to mathematics, design graphics. Will marks have to set aside for 'showing mastery of computer assisted devices'? To some extent the problem has already been faced and solved by mathematics teachers in the case of electronic calculators. What is new, however, is that the computer assistance is coming at the Output, and public, end of the teaching-learning process rather than at the Processing phase.

CAL function No. 19: enables the learner to produce high-quality forms of representation.

Summary

Schooling is a social experience during which, it is intended, individuals grow to maturity learning those values, attitudes and habits which constitute civilised society. Traditional classroom teaching may be seen as an expression of an intuitive sense of what is worthwhile in a deep moral sense. At its best, traditional 'chalk and talk' inducts the learner in countless subtle and pervasive manners of proceeding. The teacher acts as master practioner, leading novitiates through the discipline of the subject towards mastery and subsequently towards feelings of competence, confidence and community. Much of what a teacher does happens not in a formal classroom context but in the casual human interactions that make up the school day. Teaching, it could be said, is not concerned primarily with the transmission of information. It is, above all else, a means by which human values are experienced, shared and developed.

If this is true, what place has CAL in the curriculum? We have explored what it can do. But what is its value? At the moment it seems to be effective for teaching a wide range of facts, empirical concepts and procedural skills. Used in conjunction with other activities, especially discussion, it may also serve the social and ethical purposes of the school. CAL will continue to occupy more time in the curriculum, but more important than its instrumental assistance to learning is its power to help us re-conceptualise the role of the teacher. We can hope that the teacher's 'industrial role' – as foreman to the drudgery of fact gathering and skill practice – will be seen as insignificant compared to the central and more honourable role of adult guide to the young in finding meanings, purpose and values in growing up. When that has been achieved, the Structural question with which this chapter began will have been addressed and answered.

Note

1. 'Computer' may be taken throughout as a shorthand reference to the computer, its programs and related peripherals.

References

Adams, A., and Jones, E. (1983), *Teaching Humanities in the Microelectronic Age*. Milton Keynes: Open University Press.

Bruner, J. S. (1967), *Studies in Cognitive Growth*. Chichester: Wiley.

— (1973), *Beyond the Information Given*. London: Allen and Unwin.

Hartley, J. R. (1981), 'Appraisal of computer-assisted learning in the U.K.', in N. J. Rushby, ed. (1981).

Kemmis, S. Atkin, R. and Wright, E. (1977), *How do Students Learn?* Occasional Paper No. 5, University of East Anglia: Centre of Applied Research in Education.

Maddison, J. (1983), *Education in the Microelectronic Era*. Milton Keynes: Open University Press.

Papert, S. (1981), *Mindstorms: Children, Computers and Powerful Ideas*. Brighton: Harvester Press.

Rowntree, D. (1982), *Educational Technology in Curriculum Development*. New York: Harper and Row.

Rushby, N. J., James, E. B., and Anderson, J. S. A. (1981), 'A Three-dimensional view of computer-based learning in continental Europe', in N. J. Rushby, ed. (1981).

Rushby, N. J. (ed.) (1981), *Selected Readings in Computer-based Learning*. London: Kogan Page.

3. Cognitive demand and CAL

JEAN D. M. UNDERWOOD

Fact: there is at least one microcomputer in the majority of UK schools. Assumption: some good will come of it.

The majority of schools have now installed a microcomputer, and for many teachers it is a challenging experience. Buying a micro has been a major act of faith for head teachers, who must now be eager for the educational benefits to accrue. As Clark (1984: 2) points out, the search for a technology to revolutionise teaching is not a new phenomenon: 'It seems that each new technological development for storing and delivering information rekindles the hope that we will increase the learning outcomes more than "older" media'. It is very easy, however, to mistake sophisticated technology for sophisticated learning, assuming productive outcomes when students communicate with computers. The use of the computer in distance learning is a case in point (see Freeman, 1984). This chapter, in discussing the experiences of the author and an associated group of teachers working in primary schools (age range five to eleven years), will provide some tentative evidence of the educational benefits of the classroom computer.

The programs selected for discussion can, used well, make high cognitive demands on the user, often emphasising the processes by which a goal is achieved rather than any final answer. Optimal, or near optimal, use of such programs not only stretches the child, it also places a heavy strain on the teacher, demanding flexibility of thought and an ever-increasing range of knowledge and skills. It also raises questions about the criteria for evaluating such work. In attempting to identify the nature of such demands on teachers, key questions as to the adequacy of our initial and in-service training are highlighted, and these form the final discussion point of this chapter.

The computer: teacher or tool?

The success of micros in the classroom is not assured. Indeed, Chandler (1984: 1) suggests that this powerful tool has made it possible for educational practice to take a giant step backwards into the nineteenth century, because it is 'the ultimate weapon of those who want to get "back to Basics" '. Rubin (1983) echoes the complaint that the micro is being used to develop low-level sub-skills in reading and language, with an emphasis on practice and rote learning. This is due partly to the nature of the computer, which encourages a mechanistic, detail-oriented education, focusing on 'correct' or un-ambiguous answers; but also to the ease with which work cards and books, concentrating on sub-skills, are converted into programs.

Many workers would argue that the computer can and should be used in more liberating and creative ways rather than as a practice (beware the word 'teaching') machine (Chandler, 1983; Papert, 1981; Wilkinson and Patterson, 1983). Papert has argued eloquently against its use as a 'teaching' machine, suggesting that such a powerful technology can open up new fields of knowledge and encourage the development of higher-level cognitive skills.

The debate on what we should do with computers in the classroom will probably rumble on for a good few years yet, and not all teachers will resolve the question in the same way. O'Shea and Self (1983) emphasise the bewildering array of opinions as to the role of educational computers. At the same time, like Chandler, they are disturbed by the moves to a more mechanistic education supported by much of the available computer software. For, as they say, it is not that it is wrong to practise sub-skills – indeed, such practice is vital (Underwood and Underwood, 1984) – but that if that is all there is to education, then it is severely impoverished.

Although there is wide support for using computers in a variety of ways in the classroom and, as Bork (1984) comments, no single philosophy of education should limit the choices available, this chapter is concerned with those uses of the computer which are designed to place higher cognitive demands on children. In the terms of Bloom's taxonomy (1956) we are discussing programs which go beyond the acquisition and comprehension of knowledge, encouraging children to apply skills and knowledge, to evaluate or make judgements, and finally to draw together disparate information into a whole, in order to solve a given problem. Such programs encourage the child to use the computer as a tool, particularly a tool to amplify his own thinking rather than as a teacher or tester. Two main themes will be developed, the first of which queries whether there is any evidence to suggest that the use of the computer can achieve such elevated aims as encouraging the development of higher cognitive skills? Clark (1984) argues that the evidence, to date, is highly controversial and that supposed learning from CAL can be attributed to uncontrolled effects of content, instructional method and novelty. Secondly, if we are moving away from a fact-oriented towards a process-oriented curriculum, what are the implications for teachers in training and for established staff in the classroom?

Cognitive demand and educational outcomes

The most easily identified uses of the computer as a tool are those seen in operation in the world outside the classroom, namely data processing and word processing. The educational value set on information retrieval skills is demonstrated by the range of data base packages, such as *Factfile*, *Microquest* and *Inform 2*, which are available for schools. The ready acceptance of the usefulness of such software reflects an established awareness of the need to develop information-handling skills as highlighted in key reports such as Bullock (1975). Although many workers argue that the word-processor is also an important tool for stimulating children's thinking and language (Chandler, 1984; Daiute and Taylor, 1981; Levin *et al.*, 1983), there is some evidence – for example, the DTI's lack of support for printers in primary schools – that the educational value of word processing is less widely appreciated than that of information processing. Our first study will therefore concentrate on two information handling programs, *Factfile* and *Seek*.

Developing classificatory skills

Factfile, part of the MEP Micro Primer Pack, is a data base specifically designed 'as a gentle introduction to the storage and retrieval of data on a microcomputer' (Chandler, 1984: 18). It has many features of a standard commercial data base in which information is displayed along two dimensions, the record and the field. *Seek*, and its accompanying programs *Think* and *Intree*, allow children to build a binary classification tree from their own data, which they or other children can then interrogate or extend. *Seek*, and similar programs such as *Animal* and *Tree of knowledge*, are viewed as 'learning games' (Chandler, 1984) rather than as data bases, because they lack the essential ability to sort. In developing files for both *Factfile* and *Seek*, children need to make decisions about the nature of the information available to them. In coming to understand that the structure of the file governs what we may ask, they may indeed acquire a sophisticated and valuable skill.

Each of us, whether child or adult, makes sense of a body of data by sorting that information into groups of like things. Skills of classification, or categorisation, are basic but high-level skills, involving a range of sub-skills, including observation and discrimination plus the ability to see patterns in the world. All these are vital to cognitive development (see Bruner *et al.*, 1956; Mayer, 1983; Rosch, 1978). As both *Factfile* and *Seek* are essentially classificatory programs, it might be presumed that their use by children would have a beneficial effect on the ability to complete a range of classificatory tasks. Underwood and Brawn (in preparation) found that in a pre/post classificatory test situation children who had used either *Factfile* or *Seek* as part of a three-week project on the topic of 'Cheeses' performed consistently better than a matched group of children who had not developed their data bases on the computer. In particular, children in the computer-user groups used an increasing number of constraint-seeking questions, rather than specific questions, when involved in a post-test 'Twenty Questions'-type classificatory game. The increase in such constraining questions, in the post-test situation, was reliably smaller for the non-computer group, although the organisation and classification of information were an integral part of the work done by all the children. This improvement was not a function of uncontrolled novelty, for all groups of children were given extensive experience with the computer. Only the experimental groups used data base programs, however.

The improved test performance by the computer groups was independent of age and ability, although it must be said that the most able and the least able students benefited rather less from the use of the computer than the majority of the children. In the case of the most able students a ceiling effect was apparent, while the least able were not at a high enough stage of development to benefit from the model of data organisation presented by the computer. It is not possible to say whether the gains made by those children using the computer were due to the nature of the *Factfile* or *Seek* programs, that is, the precision of data handling required in their use, or whether, motivated by the computer, children were better able to maintain task concentration. Such questions may prove extremely difficult to answer but many of us, as teachers, will be content to know that the computer does improve performance.

In line with Clark's findings, however, children in the computer groups did not out-perform children in the non-computer groups on a test designed to assess the recall of factual information acquired during the period of the project. In this situation the learning of factual information was related to measures of verbal and non-verbal intelligence (not age), with the strongest relationship being between recall and reading ability.

A premise which finds ready acceptance, among practising teachers and educational theorists alike, is that the child's educational performance will improve, over a wide range of measures, if the educational experience builds upon the child's own experiences. The use of programs such as *Factfile* and *Seek* draws strength from this view. A number of workers (Adams and Jones, 1983; Chandler, 1984; Stewart, 1984) have demonstrated the many ways such programs can be used to structure information gained from the children's or teachers' own research activities. Work completed by a group of primary school teachers, in collaboration with the author, highlights the diversity of topics that can benefit from the use of such programs. Eight teachers produced not only the more obvious data bases related to 'Myself' or 'Planets' (following current educational broadcasts) but more explorative studies of 'Endangered British animals', 'Sound in the environment' and 'Road safety'.

Each of these data bases was constructed with active help from the schoolchildren. The project on 'Myself' was developed by a teacher working with six- and seven-year-olds. In this case the teacher controlled the structure of the data base, but the children entered their own data samples at the keyboard – a task they completed with great aplomb and considerable enthusiasm. The sense of 'owning' part of the data base appeared to have a particularly strong motivating effect.

In both the 'Sound' and the 'Road safety' projects, upper junior school children were actively involved in controlling the structure of the data base. For the 'Sound' project this often led to field entries which did not exploit the full potential of the *Factfile* program. Such entries included an inability to maintain congruency of command (see Carroll, 1982; Underwood, 1983): for example, the production of the sound would be attributed to the object making the noise in the case of a car but to the human operating the object in the case of a drill or a piano. There was also a strong resistance to any form of numerical coding, despite teacher encouragement. This coding system, despite its advantages in sorting activities, presents the material in a more abstract and less understandable form, and it does not seem surprising that the children were unwilling to let go the immediacy of a descriptive field entry.

The children devising the 'Road safety' data base did use numerical and abbreviated entries, however. For example, in categorising certain road junctions close to their school as heavily used or not, they employed a five-point scale of use; 1 represented a junction with low flow and no commercial traffic and 5 a junction with lots of commercial traffic. The children came to accept the need for such coding after several fruitless attempts at accessing information from the program. Their information was too complex to be put succinctly into the program because of the number of criteria used. They made an important breakthrough in their understanding of the way in which both data bases and computers are to be used effectively. In the latter case they came to appreciate that the computer is to be used with other tools, in this case work sheets displaying a full explanation of each field structure. Secondly they learned that you often have to collapse or even throw information away in order to pick out essential patterns.

One final example may highlight that this is no easy task. One of the teachers, a perceptive and caring worker, collated the information on endangered species. As the project progressed his enthusiasm for the topic appeared to increase, but after the Easter recess this enthusiasm had largely evaporated. The cause was quite simply the inadequacy of the program. The teacher felt that he, and his pupils, would have been more successful using traditional data bases and stores, that is, books and the school library. The failure on his data base was a failure to understand that the computer sorts by literal matching and is unintelligent; thus the field 'predators' is ill served by complex entries such as – fox: badger: man: fox and badger: man and fox: –. Several fields were similarly constructed, effectively negating the computer's power to search and to provide the answers to questions that the teacher knew were available in the data base.

Data bases are seen by many as one of the most effective ways of using a computer in school. Firstly, because such programs use the full potential of the machine itself, as in the adult world, information processing by computer allows rapid and complex manipulations of data. Secondly, the opportunity for children to collate material from their own environment, plus the growing realisation that facts change and are not permanent throughout our lives, may go some way to answer Weisenbaum's (1976) concern that the computer encourages the divorce of human's from the real world.

Developing hypothesis testing skills

The use of information handling packages will not guarantee educationally beneficial results. In quizzing the data base, it is suggested, even young children can begin to ask 'good' questions and be introduced to a hypothesis-testing-strategy approach to learning. In using the 'Myself' data base our infant children were testing the relationships between colour of hair and colour of eyes, and between child height and shoe size. Subjective judgement suggests that it was a successful learning experience. The questions children ask, however, are often searching for confirmatory evidence. Thus our infants asked the computer to find all the children with blue eyes and blond hair. At such a young age they can be forgiven for not asking for those cases which would test the rule, particularly as the limited screen information presented, after a sort with *Factfile*, encourages hypothesis confirmation rather than hypothesis-testing through attempted disconfirmation.

Children also show this tendency to look for supportive rather than disconfirmatory evidence when playing explorative games such as *Mary Rose* or *Philosopher's quest*. Chandler points out that, although this is also true of adult scientists (Popper, 1968), as teachers we should be challenging rather than reinforcing such problem-solving strategies. While it seems obvious that we should agree, the pragmatics of achieving such a goal are far from clear. In the first place, how are teachers to instil in their children an approach to learning that – the work of Popper (1966) and of Wason and

Johnson-Laird (1972), in their 'Four-card trick' experiments suggests – they themselves may have great difficulty in employing? As with much of the work connected with computers, it may be easier for children to develop these 'new' ways of thinking than for the teacher. Exploration of the more progressive mathematical programs, such as *Jane* and *Diagonals*, on initial and in-service teacher courses, confirms that adults have difficulty in using a mode of thinking which employs hypothesis-testing.

Jane was one of the earliest but nevertheless most creative pieces of software available to schools. The program, developed to focus the child's attention on the basic mathematical operations of adding and multiplying, requires the child to work out what *Jane*, or one of her friends, is 'doing' to a number the child has presented to her. *Jane* takes the number 3, from the left-hand box, and passes it to the right-hand box, where a question mark appears. The child is forced to guess what the new number can be. One of several strategies can be employed, from 'I'll choose my favourite numbers' to 'I'll go along the keyboard until I've got it right'. The latter strategy, because of its consistency, is highly productive. Once it is established that *Jane* converts 3 into 6, the child has information to guide his next answer. *Jane*, given the number 4, may produce the answer 7 or 8. The child can explore these two alternatives, or, if he has yet to see any pattern, he may continue guessing until the pattern becomes obvious to him.

Many children of primary age have used this program successfully (Burkhardt, 1979). Initial responses by our adult population were less fruitful, however. One group of eighteen-year-olds appeared paralysed by fear at the thought of having to guess. It was difficult to convince them that the 'right answer', that is, the number in the right-hand box, was important only in that it gave information about the process in operation. Those of us brought up in a fact-oriented curriculum, where right answers are all-important, are necessarily disoriented in a world where there may be more than one answer to a problem, as in the world outside the classroom! One of Papert's strongest arguments for the use of *Logo* is this release from the tyranny of correctness, and the move forward to multiple solutions to problems, a thought we shall return to later in this chapter.

Diagonal is also a mathematical rule-testing game. In this program the child is presented with a rectangular grid and has to decide how many of the one-unit squares the diagonal will pass through. Again the child has control of the problem in that he can set the grid size, which allows him to test his hypothesis. Experience shows that this is easier said than done. Our primary teacher group, even though aware of the need to test rules, found themselves in a spiral of confirmatory evidence. Having established the rule that the number of squares crossed was equal to the length of the rectangle minus one plus the width minus one, they set out to test the rule using increasingly large grids. In choosing their grid sizes they appeared to be inexorably drawn to prime numbers such as 13, 17 and 23. Although each grid confirmed the rule they had established, one teacher felt increasingly unhappy about it; a gut feeling that things were all too easy made her question the group's success. On trying the test sub-routine, the members of the group were dismayed to find that their hypothesis did not fit all the test cases. It proved extremely difficult for them to let go of their hypothesis, despite the contrary evidence, and to come to use both the evidence of the test and an analysis of their own trials to form a new rule related to HCF.

This experience suggests that teachers themselves need practice with the more explorative approaches to learning. They too need to be aware of the pitfalls of looking for supportive evidence. As children have less to unlearn, they may well adapt to new approaches more readily than we teachers. Playing games is a more natural activity for children than for adults. *L – a mathematical adventure*, a new program by the ATM, may be more readily accepted by teenagers steeped in the culture of adventure and arcade games than by teachers, whose experience of this genre of leisure activities is limited.

Problem-solving and beyond

The programs discussed so far are involved with the organisation of information and hypothesis-testing, and they encourage the child to problem-solve. The final program, *Think links*, has a strong element of design. De Bono (1978: 247) regards design as a higher-level skill than problem-solving, because 'Design is more open-ended than problem-solving. It requires more creativity'.

For de Bono the open-endedness of design extends the child beyond the specific goal orientation of problem-solving. Whether design is one element of, or an extension beyond, problem-solving, it is a worthwhile educational activity. In *Think links* children's ability to design is developed through a series of increasingly complex activities. Initially children are asked to classify, by various criteria, five randomly selected objects presented by the computer. For example, they may have to grade the following on the criterion of softness: matches, a shoe, water, a spade and a table. This encourages children to view objects in new ways. The second phase of the game is to use five such objects to solve a specific problem such as crossing a stream, catching a fish or getting into the house, having lost the key. Finally the child is asked to invent or design a device to sort potatoes or catch a dog.

It is not necessary to use *Think links* to encourage lateral thinking. Indeed, the primary teacher using this program had operated a de Bono-type science course for several years. He nevertheless found it a useful addition to his science activities. The children, aged between ten and eleven years, many from deprived backgrounds and with a range of learning difficulties, responded well to the computer problems. Figure 1(a) shows the solution to an escaped bear in a shopping arcade, and figure 1(b) is a design for a mousetrap.

The use of the program, while not essential to the children's course of scientific inquiry, added to their work in two ways. Firstly it was an extensive source of problems and puzzles and thus a boon to the teacher. Secondly, the children were presented with random materials to work with, some of which might be irrelevant to the task in hand. This element of redundancy, so much part of life, is carefully screened out of most problems we present to children. We all have a tendency to give them the most appropriate tools for the job and no more. We tend not to stimulate skills of selection.

Teacher training and the computer in the classroom

An initial premise of this chapter was that there are more exciting things to do with the micro in the classroom than drill and practice activities. The examples of micro use presented here suggest that there are programs available which are skills-oriented and can stretch children's minds. All these programs actively encourage problem-solving and, while the data bases operate within the child's measurable world, others allow the child to enter a creative, and at times, fantastic world.

The use of the computer as a tool will test the teacher's organisational skills. Equally, many of our exemplar programs require considerable factual knowledge or conceptual understanding. For teachers, however, the most demanding element of such

(a) You get the clock and hypnotise the bear and to make shore the bear stays hypnatised put a mirror in front of him so that he stares into his own eyes and then put a saucepan over his mouth to stop him biting and then use the telephone to phone the zoo

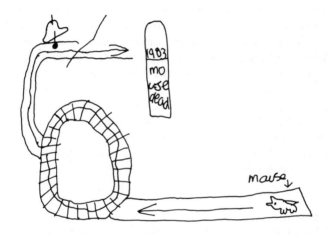

(b) The mouse runs along the wood round the weel up the road ring the bell. scwot the mouse-grave ready.

Fig. 1. Two examples of children's work using the *Think links* program.
(a) *Problem*: recapture an escaped bear in the supermarket. *Materials provided*: clock, telephone, saucepan, mirror. By Darcy, aged ten years.
(b) *Problem*: design a mousetrap. By Tamma, aged ten years.

programs is the emphasis on the processes of thinking rather than on facts or final solutions. This begs the question of how to evaluate the work produced. What are the criteria for assessing the two pieces of work shown in fig. 1? Functionality, perhaps. But the questions were often fanciful. Use of all materials? But recognising redundancy is a skill to be cultivated and one that the least able in our groups were struggling to acquire. Novelty, perhaps? But should we applaud an inefficient solution? The answer will probably lie with the teacher's own objectives for using such a program; functionality will be praised by some but not by others.

Teachers do need to be given a forum for discussing these conflicting criteria of evaluation, and here may be one useful role for initial and in-service courses. Discussions will be most beneficial if the teachers come to value thinking more than knowing. With the restrictions of the secondary school examination system and, the 'return to basics' movement at primary level, this is not a hopeful time for such developments. Nevertheless, there must be opportunities for teachers to explore their own thinking and evaluate their own problem-solving skills. There are opportunities available to the colleges as they design their 'Twenty-hour computer literacy courses', in accord with DES requirements. Such courses should emphasis the computer as a catalyst to more powerful thinking, and minimise its role as teacher.

References

Adams, A., and Jones, E. (1983), *Teaching Humanities in the Microelectronic Age*. Milton Keynes: Open University Press.

Bloom, B. (1956), *Taxonomy of Educational Objectives*. Handbook 1, *Cognitive Domain*. New York: Mackay.

Bork, A. (1984), 'Computers and the future: education', in P. R. Smith (ed.), *Cal 83*. Oxford: Pergamon Press.

de Bono, E. (1978), *Lateral Thinking*. London: Penguin.

Bruner, J., Goodnow, J. J., and Austin, G. A. (1956), *A Study of Thinking*. New York: Wiley.

Bullock Report (1975), *A Language for Life*. London: HMSO.

Burkhardt, H. (1979), 'Let's look at Jane', *Itma Newsletter*, 2, 18–28.

Carroll, J. M. (1982), 'Learning, using and designing command paradigms', *Human Learning*, 1, 31–62.

Chandler, D. (1984), *Young Learners and the Microcomputer*. Milton Keynes: Open University Press.

Clark, R. E. (1984), 'Learning From Computers: Theoretical Problems'. Paper presented at the AERA annual meeting, New Orleans.

Daiute, C., and Taylor, R. (1981), 'Computers and Improvement of Writing'. Paper presented to the ACM conference.

Freeman, R. (1984), 'MAIL Aided Learning', in P. R. Smith (ed.), *Cal 83*. Oxford: Pergamon Press.

Levin, J. A., Boruta, M. J., and Vasconcellos, M. T. (1983), 'Microcomputer-based environments for writing: a writer's assistant', in A. C. Wilkinson, (ed.), *Classroom Computers and Cognitive Science*. New York: Academic Press.

Mayer, R. E. (1983), *Thinking, Problem Solving, Cognition*. New York: Freeman.

O'Shea, T., and Self, J. (1983), *Learning and Teaching with Computers*. Brighton: Harvester Press.

Papert, S. (1981), *Mindstorms: Children, Computers and Powerful Ideas*. Brighton: Harvester Press.

Popper, K. R. (1966), *The Logic of Scientific Discovery*. London: Hutchinson.

Rosch, E. H. (1978), 'Principles of categorisation', in E. H. Rosch and B. B. Lloyd (eds.), *Cognition and Categorisation*. Hillside, N. J.: Erlbaum.

Rubin, A. (1983), 'The computer confronts language arts: cans and shoulds for education', in A. C. Wilkinson (ed.), *Classroom Computers and Cognitive Science*. New York: Academic Press.

Stewart, J. (1984), *Building – in your Ideas:* Module 4. London: Longman Micro Software.

Underwood, G. and J. D. M. (1984), 'Cognitive processes in reading and spelling', in A. Cashdan (ed.), *Teaching Literacy*. Oxford: Blackwell.

Underwood, J. D. M. (1983), 'Analysing command language paradigms in software for computer-assisted learning', *Human Learning*, 2, 7–16.

Watson, P. C., and Johnson-Laird, P. N. (1972), *Psychology of Reasoning*. London: Batsford.

Weisenbaum, J. (1976), *Computer Power and Human Reason*. San Francisco: W. H. Freeman.

Wilkinson, A. C., and Patterson, J. (1983), 'Issues at the interface of theory and practice', in A. C. Wilkinson (ed.) *Classroom Computers and Cognitive Science*. New York: Academic Press.

Software

(all programs are currently available for the BBC microcomputer): *Animal* (1983), Tecmedia. *Diagonal* (1983), Muse. *Factfile* (1982), Cambridge Microsoftware. *Inform 2* (1983), Nottinghamshire County Council. *Jane* (1983), Longman. *L – a mathemagical adventure* (1984), ATM. *Mary Rose* (1982), Ginn. *Microquest* (1983), Tecmedia. *Seek* (1084), Longman. *Think links* (1983), Anita Straker. *Tree of knowledge* (1982), Acornsoft.

Acknowledgements

This chapter is supported by the able work of the following teachers: E. A. Coglan, R. M. Dawson, J. Downes, J. B. Harrop, R. Heeley, A. Heydon, B. M. Morrison, J. E. Train, J. B. Weatherill.

4. Microcomputer use

A case study

T. EWEN and A. ROBERTS

The chapter is based on a survey of microcomputer use in six upper schools; its aim is to assess the extent to which schools are preparing their pupils for a place in a computer-based society. The presuppositions are that (a) there will be pervasive changes in society emanating from the implementation and advancement of technology based on micro-electronics; (b) society will expect schools to have anticipated these changes and prepared their pupils accordingly.

The proposed 'ideal preparation' is an activity profile which is essential only to the assessments made in this chapter. No other intrinsic merit is claimed for it, although we consider it compatible both with the cognitive and structural theories that frame the learning process in schools and with the conventional hierarchy of learning objectives, namely imparting basic knowledge, establishing basic ideas and concepts, developing the use of abstraction and hypothesis, encouraging understanding and the formation of informed attitudes.

There are four categories of activity in the proposed ideal preparation, and these are termed 'instructional', 'revelatory', 'conjectural' and 'emancipatory' (Rushby, 1979).

The ideal preparation defined by categories of activity

These categories of activity are regarded as appropriate experience of the use of microcomputers in schools. There is no sequential requirement but there is obviously a gradient in terms of both difficulty and maturity. The categories have been defined by selecting appropriate activities or uses of the following manner.

Instructional category

Following an elementary introduction to the microcomputer, the machine would be used for drill and practice. Only simple programs in any subject are required, and the learning process is directed towards elementary knowledge and skills. Keyboard dexterity, comprehension and interpretation of the visual display would be consolidated alongside the subject diet. Games could be used to reinforce or indeed initiate the interfacing with the microcomputer but, in view of their limited educational endowment, not to an excessive extent.

Revelatory category

Here the objective is to strengthen the grasp of ideas and concepts. Programs based on simulation are apposite in this context, and some may generate data amenable to graphical interpretation.

The control function of microcomputers, as illustrated by simple event sequencing, is highly relevant to the topical need for industrial relevance, and this might be exemplified, for example, by the sequencing of lights in a doll's house or the management of a model train set.

Computer programming is included in this category. The level of attainment in this activity is determined in most schools by examination requirements, consequently no level of competence is specified as a requirement of ideal preparation.

Computer-assisted learning, in any subject, above the drill and practice level qualifies for inclusion in the revelatory category, though many exisiting programs depend on simulation, already considered.

Conjectural category

The tasks are now chosen to encourage thought rather than mere assimilation, and the emphasis is on uses which entail the manipulation and analysis of data, the use of abstractions and the testing of ideas or hypotheses. The envisaged repertoire embraces several types of program of the following kinds.

Data base, when data are collected or available, e.g. weather forecasts, census or poll results, population figures, etc. These data are processed in ways which organise or manage information and discern patterns or trends.

Analysis of data from simulated experiments, which involves generating results by computer and analysing them to discover the underlying operating relationship (e.g. Boyle's law). The data can frequently be arranged in or transformed to a linear form so that the pupil may use graphing and graphical interpretation.

Hypothesis, based on the testing of hypotheses or ideas. This activity may be the extended form of data analysis or an integral part of the approach to such analysis. Thus a prediction founded on theoretical insights can be compared with the 'reality' stored in the computer as a test of the truth (correctness) or usefulness of the theory.

When the pupil has experience of different microcomputer uses it becomes appropriate to discuss ideas such as capacity, versatility, limitations and the implications of these as part of a computer appreciation course, by which time it is opportune to begin to draw attention to some of the broader social implications of computer intrusion.

Emancipatory category

In this category of activities the emphasis is on understanding the broader contextual influences of microprocessors. The micro-processor itself can be used by the pupil in only a limited emancipatory way, for example in work-load reduction, when the computer is used as a subsidiary tool in engaging a comprehensive subject. Probably this would take the form of a mathematical process (e.g. a statistical package), but the wider the experience of the subjugation of the computer to the designs of individual enterprise the more cohesive the educational effect.

Beyond the direct use of the microcomputer there should be other emancipatory activities. These could include assignments or project work which allows the pupil to investigate in greater depth one or more computer-related issues, e.g. the cashless society, computer files and personal privacy, skill obsolescence and retraining, the need for adaptability, microtechnology and unemployment, job sharing and extended leisure time, etc. This would provide practice in gaining access to information sources, pruning back excessive information by judicious selection, and using the residue to the best effect in informed reporting.

The systems approach, as a means of appreciating the interactive loops which connect events and changes that might otherwise be seen only in isolation could also be introduced into discussions of computer-induced change. Furthermore the changes that might conceivably follow from a given set of circumstances could be examined by pupils using systems analysis as a framework for their conjectures.

By now signs of divergent thinking and the formation of informed opinions and attitudes should become evident. The educational canvas is beginning to have cultural rather than simply instrumental dimensions, and receptive pupils would have the greatest potential for later influencing the commercial and political control which might otherwise be shaped by narrow utilitarian or ideological minds.

Finally, having set out the referential categories of activity used to assess the effective preparation provided by a school, Table 1 brings them together in summary form. Pupils achieving the full span of these activities would be sufficiently informed to face the computer-induced changes in society with a degree of confidence whatever the nature of their subsequent education and/or career.

The content of Table 1 may seem perversely academic for schools functioning in the present educational climate, but the appearance may be more semantic than real. Certainly many of the activities were observed in the case-study schools used. The essential theme is simply that the pupil should be exposed to and become familiar with a variety of computer functions in a spread of subject areas. Equally, the pupil should be made aware of and possibly come to understand the implications of computer applications for the individual and society as a whole. Hence the skein of pupil preparation outlined in Table 1 to which has been made in the assessment of a school's achievement.

The procedures used in each case study included an initial

Table 1 Summary of categories of activity

Category type	Contributing activity
(a) Instructional	Drill/Practice Games
(b) Revelatory	Simulation Control function Programming (basics)
(c) Conjectural	Data base Data analysis Hypothesis Implications (of the computer)
(d) Emancipatory	Work load reduction Project work (investigative) Systems approach (to change) Systems analysis (of change)

interview with the Head, leading to agreed arrangements for subsequent visits; a questionnaire, completed in consultation with the Head and other members of staff as necessary; full-day visits spent with the computer studies specialist and any other subject specialists using the microcomputer in their teaching; observations of break and lunchtime computer use; a schedule of revisits the following term to review the sampling of a school's activities.

The questionnaire covered items such as computing resources (staff, equipment, software), an outline of computer use in the school, school policy on computers, and activities (as listed in Table 1) taking place in the school. The details recorded on the questionnaire were tested against the direct observation and critical judgement of the assessor.

Satisfactory coverage of a specific category of activity (Instructional, etc.) was not necessarily dependent on achieving all the activities but rather on whether, in the assessor's judgement, the school did enough, with sufficient commitment, to be classed as satisfactory in that one category.

The observed computer activities for each school are summarised below and, for convenient comparison, in Table 2.

School I

Games: played by computer studies sixth-formers during break (which should be devoted to project work).

Simulation: in the form of a commercial genetic engineering program used as a teaching aid in Biology.

Programming: as part of O level computer studies (taken in the sixth form in this school).

Implications: as part of O level computer studies a pupil can examine a computer application which is of particular individual interest.

School II

Drill/practice: using programs devised by staff in different subjects (maths, stats, chemistry, physics).

Simulation: for example, a program created by the chemistry master illustrating the experimental determination of water hardness by titration.

Programming: as part of O level computer studies.

Data base, data analysis: a statistical program based on a word-length examination of a piece of prose leading to distribution and cumulative histograms and curve approximating the results.

Implications: as part of a lower sixth-form computer appreciation course designed by the school's computing co-ordinator.

School III

Games: played during lunch break to encourage an introduction to microcomputers.

Programming: as part of O level computer studies.

Hypothesis: as part of a physics program dealing with projectile trajectories – the pupil is required, with teacher prompting, to hypothesise the relationship describing the trajectory.

School IV

Drill/practice: used to learn simple programming routines.

Simulation: as part of A level computer studies the pupils are encouraged actually to create simulations related to other subjects (physics, maths and art); this has included pattern generation and image animation in art graphics.

Programming: as part of O and A level computer studies.

Implications: as part of A level computer studies pupils are expected to create programs based on individual interests, for example *Airline Booking*.

School V

Drill-practice: chemical formulae program (produced by O level computer studies pupils).

Programming: as part of CSE/O level computer studies.

Data analysis: velocity and acceleration formulae derived from experimental data (a program devised by O level computer studies pupils).

School VI

Games: occasionally played, not encouraged.

Drill/practice: some maths programs which reinforce normal exposition.

Simulation: a physics program dealing with radioactive decay.

Control: active projects (for selected pupils only) designed to integrate electronics/computer programming/design and craft technology.

Programming: as part of BEC computer studies.

Data base: transposition of experimental data in physics.

Data analysis: analysis of variables affecting the refraction of light (physics).

Implications: as part of BEC computer studies and non-examinable sixth-form course on computer programming and appreciation.

An overview of each school was prepared leading to an assessment of its achievement. Preparation achievement is viewed both as the degree to which the school covers the four categories of activity and as the percentage of the school's intake which benefit from this degree of coverage. Of equal importance is that there is also an estimate of the percentage of pupils who leave the school without using a microcomputer or seeing one in use in any meaningful way.

School I (NOR 1,300; pupil/staff ratio 16·5)

This inner-city multiracial school has two 8K microcomputers and just one computer-trained member of staff, who is head of Maths. The software library contains thirty-four programs, which include six project tapes produced by students, eleven games and seventeen educational tapes from the central LEA computer library. Only the games and one educational tape are used regularly. The school provides a two-year O level examination course in computer studies, but this is an option taken in the lower and upper sixth. Typically there might be six pupils in each year of the course, and break-time access to the computer is confined to those doing computer project work (though some games are played). By the time this group reaches the upper sixth they are likely to have some conception of the implications of computer technology – but the group comprises less than 2 per cent of the school-leavers and its activity is confined to computing.

This small percentage is consonant with the school policy of concentrating on the O level examination option. Hoever, as and when extra resources become available there are plans to expand the present work, introduce computer appreciation to the fifth form and

Table 2 Summary of computer activities

Activity	Category												
	Instructional		Revelatory		Conjectural				Emancipatory				
	Games	D/P	Sim.	Con.	Prog.	Data base	Data anal.	Hyp.	Impl.	Wk. Redn.	Inv.	Syst. view	Syst. anal.
I	(*)	–	*	–	○	–	–	–	(*)	–	–	–	–
II	–	*	*	–	○	*	*	–	(*)	–	–	–	–
III	*	–	(*)	–	○	–	–	*	–	–	–	–	–
IV	–	*	–	–	○△	–	(*)	–	(*)	–	–	–	–
V	–	(*)	*	–	○	–	*	–	–	–	–	–	–
VI	*	*	*	*	△	*	*	–	*	–	–	–	–

Key
○ O level Computer Studies plus related project works.
△ A level Computer Studies (or BEC) plus related project work.
(*) Derived activity associated with Computer Studies project work.
★ Any other activity.

diffuse microcomputer use to other subject areas. At present about 16 per cent of the intake use a biology simulation program, which means that, at most, 18 per cent can be classified as seeing a computer in use, i.e. about 82 per cent of the intake does not, in any real sense, see a computer in use.

School II (NOR 1,200; pupil/staff ratio 18·9)

School II, which has a middle-class catchment, has three microcomputers of 8K, 16K and (in the science department) 32K capacity. There is also a disc-drive machine and a printer with graphics capability. In the software library there are about fifty-two tapes, of which only twenty, all written by members of staff, are in use. The rest, from commercial and local sources, are regarded as unacceptable in quality or irrelevant to class use. There are eleven computer-trained staff, including four specialists, and eleven others with some experience in using microcomputers. The head of computing has the responsibility of co-ordinating all computer activity throughout the school.

The school runs CSE and O level examination courses in computer studies and, in combination with microcomputer use in other areas such as maths, stats, physics, chemistry and geography, this means that approximately 20 per cent of intake effectively experience the activities comprising the Instructional, Revelatory and Conjectural categories. Any pupil may use the computers outside the timetable, but in the main games are prohibited. School policy gives priority to the computer examination options but not to the exclusion of their use in other subjects (see above). Indeed, in the lower sixth there is provision for a one-year non-examinable option in computer appreciation. As a result of this wider commitment, no pupil leaves the school at either fifth or sixth-form level without some meaningful contact with microcomputers.

School III (NOR 600; pupil/staff ratio 16·4)

This all-girl school, with a middle-class catchment, possesses one 8K microcomputer and a modern TV screen linkage. The software library contains about forty programs, obtained from the central LEA computer library, of which half are educational and the other half games. None is regarded as intrinsically educationally valuable. There are two computer-trained teachers, including the head of maths, who spends half his time as computer specialist. Only one other teacher (physics) uses the microcomputer.

The school offers CSE and O level examination courses in computer studies, but there is serious doubt about the relevance of the syllabuses, which perhaps explains why no great emphasis is placed on examination results. Neither is there a strongly acknowledged need to prepare pupils for a micro-based society and hence no plans exist to advance beyond the present level of commitment.

Consequently this school is operating essentially within the narrow CSE/O level band of computer studies with just about 10 per cent of its intake. In the light of this policy, 90 per cent of leavers have no significant contact with the microcomputer at fifth-form level, although the existence of a sixth-form physics program reduces the figure to an estimated 80 per cent.

School IV (NOR 1,250; pupil/staff ratio 16·0)

School IV has a comprehensive catchment and a computer laboratory which houses 18K and 32K microcomputers plus a line printer and a TV interface modem. Amongst the stock seventy-five tapes there are eighteen devised by the staff, twelve sixth-form project tapes, and the rest are educational tapes from the central LEA computer library. The staff contains five computer-trained teachers, including two specialists. Computer studies are established at CSE/O level, and for high achievers there is an A level option. No other computer options are available, and school policy places the emphasis on computing examinations so that at least some pupils are equipped to compete for computer-related jobs on leaving school. As a result this school operates, like school III, in a narrow computer studies band but does so with about 33 per cent of its intake.

There are plans for another 32K microcomputer with which it is intended to broaden the curricular use and launch a computer appreciation course for less academic pupils. Meanwhile, although fifteen teachers register interest in computer-assisted learning, the school's policy effectively denies them access to the present machines. Consequently there is only minor activity in other subjects (maths, physics and art). It is estimated that school-leavers at fifth and sixth-form level could be described as not having any significant contact with the microcomputer to the extent of 67 and 60 per cent respectively.

School V (NOR 1,050; pupil/staff ratio 18·4)

The school has a working-class catchment and two 8K microcomputers housed in a cupboard in the maths department. A weekly lunchtime visit to the LEA computing centre gives some pupils supplementary access to microcomputer facilities. The maths department has eleven programs, provided by the LEA's central computer library. Only two teachers are computer-trained, including the school's specialist. The school runs a CSE/O level examination course in computer studies, and lunchtime use of microcomputers is permitted for related project work. There is no other computer work, though the policy is to extend what is already done to a greater number of pupils. The school has no real enthusiasm for the present syllabuses and see the examinations merely as a means of signalling competence to prospective employers.

Computer Studies is mainly concerned with programming but related project work is deliberately oriented towards other subjects such as maths, physics and chemistry. Consequently, like schools III and IV, the school's activities are confined by the computing priority and contact with microcomputers is limited to something like 15 per cent of the intake, which means, conversely, that the remaining 85 per cent leave school unfamiliar with computer use.

School VI (NOR 1,100; pupil/staff ratio 15·7)

Located in an upper middle-class catchment area, this school has two 8K and one 32K microcomputers. The latter is quipped with disc drive and is assigned to the science department. The software library contains fifteen staff-generated programs (maths, physics and craft topics), six sixth-form project tapes, several commercial programs (which are never used) and some games from the LEA central computer library. Seven members of staff are computer-trained, including one specialist, and six other teachers are interested in using the microcomputer. The school prefers to continue with its well established sixth-form BEC Computer Studies rather than switch to the present GEC alternatives. There is a non-examinable sixth-form option called Computer Programming and Appreciation and a once-a-week informal lunchtime session in which pupils are free to engage in a combination of physics, electronics, control function and programming activities.

The school's policy is to use the microcomputers to prepare pupils for obtaining work in a computer-oriented world, and it is accepted that this will constrain, though not prevent, broader curricular use, which is currently limited to maths, physics and craft. Five categories of use are envisaged as persisting: (a) control function, (b) programming, (c) data logging/recall, (d) advanced programmable calculations, (e) experimental simulation.

To conclude, school VI is able to sustain a range of activities which spread across the Instructional, Revelatory and Conjectural categories and involve approximately 37 per cent of its intake. Furthermore the lateral spread of microcomputer use is sufficient to ensure that no pupil leaves without some familiarity with computers. The results from the case studies were as follows.

Table 3 Summary of status of schools' preparation

School	Categories covered	% intake involved	% intake epg. no CC	Other subject use
VI	1, 2, 3	37	0 fifth-form 0 sixth-form	Maths, physics, craft
II	1, 2, 3	20	0 fifth-form 0 sixth-form	Maths, physics, stats, chemistry, geography
IV	Mainly CS O/A level	33	67 fifth-form 60 sixth-form	Maths, physics, art
V	Mainly CS O level	15	85 fifth-form 85 sixth-form	None
III	Mainly CS O level	10	90 fifth-form 80 sixth-form	Physics
I	Mainly CS O level	2	84 fifth-form 82 sixth-form	Biology

Key: category 1, Instructional; 2, Revelatory; 3, Conjectural; 4, Emancipatory; CS, Computer Studies; CC, Computer contact; Expg., experiencing.

School performance measured against the four categories of activity

The case studies of the computer and computer-aided work show that no school in the sample spanned the four categories which stand as an empirical representation of ideal pupil preparation for entry to a computer-oriented world. It is the Emancipatory category which is effectively absent from even the best schools in the sample. The activities in this category, in addition to the use of the computer as a tool for reducing human work load, bring an element of investigation into trends as well as a systems approach to discussing and analysing change. Although the latter activities make no demands on computer time, curricular constraints may well be sufficient to ensure their continuing exclusion from a school's repertoire. Consequently coverage of the Instructional, Revelatory and Conjectural categories is construed to be the limit of current 'best practice', particularly where the school makes efforts to cover computer appreciation and implications. Although this limit may be seen as a shortfall, it is the excess 'capacity' of the four proposed categories that allows the shortfall to manifest itself: in that sense the different performance of schools is not suppressed or limited by lack of headroom.

Ranking of school performance

As measured by the extent to which a school caters for the categories of activity discussed above, only two schools (VI and II) achieve a satisfactory status by meeting, in the authors' judgement, the requirements of the Instructional, Revelatory and Conjectural categories. The remainder, conversely, are regarded as falling short. In rounded percentages the figures for the sample are: satisfactory schools, 33 per cent; others 67 per cent.

Proportion of pupils receiving adequate preparation

Even the two high-achieving schools, VI and II, meet the stated criteria with only 37 and 20 per cent respectively of their school-leavers. From these data, the school leavers regarded as products of satisfactory preparation for the sample as a whole are only 9·5 per cent of the leaver population, i.e. less than 10 per cent. Therefore about 90 per cent of school-leavers, on the basis of the authors' criteria, may be regarded as inadequately prepared for a micro-oriented society.

Indeed, the fourth column in Table 3 means that, even taking the most favourable figures, on average 50 per cent of leavers have no meaningful interaction with microcomputers at all. Real figures are, of course, school-specific and may vary, according to the sample, from 0 to as much as 85 per cent.

Finally, on a more specific point, examination of Table 2 shows that at a time when schools are being exhorted to provide for the needs of industry, only one in six of the schools in the sample uses the microcomputer in the control function.

From an analysis of the case studies it is suggested that the schools with better overall resource levels are spanning more of the categories of activity in the referential scheme of pupil preparation. Hence in Table 4 we have summarised the known relevant resource characteristics for the schools in the sample for comparison with the measures of achievement or effectiveness shown in Table 3. Referring to both tables, it can be seen that, in a general way, upper socio-economic catchment, more trained staff and lower pupil/keyboard ratio are together associated with better attainment on all four criteria of effectiveness (Table 3). Hence the total weighted score in column 6 of Table 4, which composites the effects of 'resources' (catchment, staff and keyboard ratio), shows a qualitative correlation with measures of school effectiveness. (School III would be more noticeably 'out of line', i.e. under-achieving for its 'resource index', if the trained staff were doubled to compensate for its 'half size', i.e. NOR = 600 compared with an average NOR = 1,150 for the other five schools.)

Taking the top-ranked school VI as the best realistic model of an effective school under prevailing conditions (achieving an adequate preparation for 37 per cent of its output with seven trained staff), it could be argued that to attain comparable results (given the requisite policy and resources) the requirements for additional trained staff to bring each school up to seven would be: school II, none (it already has eleven trained staff); school IV, two; schools V and I, five each; school III, 1·5, i.e. two (after making allowance for its 'half size', NOR = 600). The sum of the extra staff would therefore be fourteen, which as a percentage of the total staff in six schools (375) is a rounded up 4 per cent.

It is also interesting to note that schools VI and II, with similar catchments and keyboard ratios (Table 4), have subject dispersions (Table 3) which relate to the number of trained staff (Table 4). Similarly, if we compare school VI (with all its relative advantages) with school IV, the rough parity of trained teachers is reflected in an equal spread to other subject areas. And again, the one influential feature which significantly favours school IV, compared with school I, III and V, is the higher number of trained staff, which corresponds with a much better dispersion of computer use in this group of four schools. In terms of untrained but interested staff there is an advantaged group – schools II, IV and VI – and a disadvantaged group – schools I, III and V (Table 4). Conceivably the higher degree of interest produces a climate which is also more favourable to computer use in other subjects.

Since one of the stated aims of the Micro-electronics Education Programme is that children should be prepared for a society in which microelectronics are commonplace and pervasive (Thorne, 1982), the

Table 4 Summary of school characteristics

1. School	2. Catchment classification	3. Pupils per keyboard	4. Trained staff [specialists]	5. Other staff interested	6. Weighted scores cols. 2, 3, 4*	Total score
VI	Upper middle	367	7 [1]	6	5, 4.6, 3.2	12.8
II	Middle	340	11 [4]	11	4, 5, 5	14.0
IV	Comprehensive	625	5[2]	15	3, 2.7, 2.3	8.0
V	Working	525	2[1]	(0)	2, 3.2, 0.9	6.1
III	Middle	600	2[1]	1	4, 2.8, 0.9	7.7
I	Inner-city multi-racial	650	2[1]	1	1, 2.6, 0.9	4.5

* Column 2, upper middle = 5; column 3, 340 = 5; column 4, 11 = 5.

school microcomputer needs to be seen as 'symbiotic' with the widest possible range of subjects. In this way the familiarisation process spreads to the non-maths/science groups, and the common association of computers with maths is attenuated or completely dissolved. Of the schools in the sample, II, IV and VI are the closest to achieving this goal.

However, individual teachers often need to be resilient and persistent, as a teacher of physics in school IV would testify on finding it almost impossible to book a machine for a specific lesson in the face of keen demand for access to the computers. On another occasion, and in other circumstances (in fact whilst looking for suitable educational programs), he borrowed six tapes from the LEA central computer library, only to find that just one worked on the school's computer – and its content was not what the title implied, anyway!

This is not an uncommon experience, nor is it unimportant. For hard-pressed teachers reliability and educational value are essential, and the failure of software, in any sense, is a direct way of generating a dismissive view of microcomputers. Many tentative approaches to their use have probably wilted in this way. Jensen (1982) rightly reminds us that it would be a mistake not to keep the distinction between medium and message in mind and that computer-assisted learning gets a bad name from bad examples of software. Indeed, in the six case-study schools it was found that just a single commercial program (excluding games) was in regular use (school I), the sole survivor of eleven tested programs. This situation may be changing, but during the study the programs in use were very largely generated in school (staff or sixth-form project tapes).

However, in-school programs can pose intractable problems, in fact one computer specialist in the study had written and rewritten programs for geography, biology and history; but no amount of consultation and refinement could produce a product acceptable to the specialist subject teachers. Whether they were expecting too much or the programmer lacked the necessary skills was not clear, but in this example there must be implications for the diversification of computer use.

From the experience of the physics teacher and the evidence of the case studies generally it is obvious that with just two or three microcomputers (and the government scheme only applied to a single purchase) there is inevitable tension between computer studies and the other subjects. The outcome is then determined either by a policy decision or by *laissez-faire*. School IV, with two computers and O and A level computing, achieves as much dispersion (Table 3) as school VI with three computers and a firm commitment to BEC computing. On the other hand school II, which also has three computers and a preference for O level computing only, is able to accommodate more curricular spread (Table 3). This school has also appointed a computer co-ordinator and this points to a policy favourable to diversification. The co-ordinator not only deflects extraneous responsibilities (e.g. technical support services) from the computer/maths department and referees competing demands for the computers but also senses the potential for new computer uses and appreciates the resources and management needs that will realise the potential. Thus we see school policy, through its selection of computer studies courses and its encouragement of alternative uses of the computer, influencing the pattern of overall use.

Table 5 shows some detail which might affect the outcome of the tension between competing uses. We have already noted other complicating factors, but in the final analysis it is the actual intensity of Computer Studies use which has to be countered. The characteristic which seems to be the operative countervailing force is the number of trained staff (Table 5), some of whom, with sufficient motivation, will pull computer use into other subjects. It is noticeable, within the sample, that the number of trained staff tends to be higher where there is an awareness of and a commitment to the wider implications of computers in the policy of the school. In this respect the schools tend to subdivide into two groups: II and VI; I, III, IV and V. Hence we see policy differences shaping the total picture.

Table 5 Subject use of microprocessors

School	CS course	CS usage	Other subject use	Trained staff
VI	BEC*	High	Maths, physics, craft	7
II	CSE/O*	High	Maths, physics, statistics, chemistry, geography	11
IV	CSE/O/ A*	High	Maths, physics, art	5
V	O*	High	None	2
III	CSE/O	Medium	Physics	2
I	O*	Medium	Biology	2

* Firmly stated policy of giving importance to computer studies.

In terms of the spread of computer use to other subjects and the number of trained staff, school II now suggests itself as the best model. Before applying this to other schools, however, it is interesting to note how school II's ratio of other subject use to trained staff, 0·45 (five subjects: eleven staff) compares with 0·43 for school VI, 0·60 for school IV and 0·50 for schools III and I, and an average of 0·50 for the five schools as a whole. (School V itself has a zero quotient.) Using the eleven trained staff of school II as the target, the additional trained staff required to achieve similar dispersion (other influences being equal) would be: school VI, five; school IV, seven; schools V, III and I, nine each; leading to a total of thirty-nine, which is approximately 10 per cent of the aggregate staff for the six schools.

We have already seen evidence of the influence of school policy at work, hence the qualifying phrases such as 'given the requisite policy' and 'other influences being equal' in the preceding discussion. As recorded in the overviews of each school and noted in Table 5, five of the six schools have a working policy which firmly commits them to a priority in the computer studies field. However, another element of policy is the recognition of a wider responsibility to the rest of the pupils to make some provision for their familiarisation with computers prior to entering fully a society increasingly pervaded by computers. On this count, as noted earlier, the schools tend to fall into two groups: one offering a wider experience of computers for more pupils; the other, for whatever reasons, tending not to make this more comprehensive provision. The group which is better endowed policy-wise tends also to be better resourced in terms of computer equipment and trained and interested staff (see the overviews and Table 4).

However, influencing teachers' interests is not a simple exercise. In school V, for example, the microcomputer was taken into the staff room on several occasions in an attempt to gain the attention of other members of staff. On each occasion the most discernible reaction was indifference rather than curiosity. Perhaps the intrusion was resented or the electronic mystique too disconcerting. Obviously interest is not so easily engendered. Which leads to the interesting supposition that, in the face of relatively new technology, in this case the microcomputer, it is indeed the teacher's attitude to innovation and change which is critical. Chambliss (1968), for example, found that personal discontent with the existing system was the most influential factor determining the adoption of innovation. Other researchers (Bishop, 1967; Bennett, 1980) have concluded that it requires one or more teachers who are dedicated to invoking new attitudes in order to achieve better attainment levels. The motivation that this implies is probably present in schools VI and II but it coexists with an overall enlightened policy and relatively good resources. High motivation is also present in school IV, but here school policy and resources are not so supportive, and the attainment is not nearly so good. Improved leadership and an extra microcomputer may be all that is needed to lift its level of attainment. In schools I and III the requisite policy, resources and attitudes are all absent, and the achievements are comparatively weak. The underprivileged catchment of school I is an additional handicap.

Before leaving the discussion of policy it is worth noting some evidence relating to girls. School VI, which has a supportive policy and working atmosphere (and good resources and catchment as well), reports a change in attitude among girls. As microelectronics becomes more established, and girls are increasingly exposed to it, related technologies, it seems, are discovered to be less daunting than imagined and therefore less stereotypically part of the male domain. As a result more girls are taking up electronics and computing in this school and many have done extremely well. In school II, however, it was noticed by direct observation that girls meeting a computer keyboard for the first time had a more hesitant approach than boys, showed greater reluctance to experiment and displayed a heightened concern about 'breaking something inside'. In the presence of boys they tended to defer to them. The observation suggests that schools might adopt a policy of segregation, at least for the introductory familiarisation sessions, in order to elicit the most favourable response from girls. The lack of achievement in the girl's school (III), alluded to earlier, would appear to be the result of the less positive attitudes and working atmosphere which derive from an indifferent school policy on computers.

The last mentioned school is in fact critical in its view of computing syllabuses but it is not alone in that. Despite the other five schools in the sample placing much importance on examinable computer studies, four have misgivings about GCE and CSE syllabuses. The common view is that they are outdated, too theoretical and inappropriate to either immediate job needs or preparation for university computing. One of the school's (VI), as a result of unusual historical development, firmly continues with its preference for BEC computer studies, which it finds more business-oriented, more applicable to the computer world, more sensitising to computer-induced change and better suited to higher education.

The importance of trained staff and school policy has been discussed but the best policy and the most highly trained staff remain ineffective unless there are the means to bring about the necessary implementation. Abstracting the best possible combination of equipment from that possessed by the schools in the sample, we have three computers, one disc drive, one printer and one TV screen linkage. Although none of the schools has exactly this combination, school II and schools VI and IV, the more effective schools, approach it most closely. Taking the above combination of equipment as a working ideal, we find that each of the following items is lacking in 67 per cent of the schools: a third computer (we have 'allocated' a second computer to school III to allow for its 'half size'), a printer, a disc drive and TV screen linkage. Each school has its own particular shortfall, but if adequate preparation crystallises to any real extent only round this size of nucleus of equipment (and the best schools in the sample could improve their rating), then it will take substantial overall investment in equipment to remedy the situation. In the case of schools which provide no real interaction with computers for large members of their pupils (see Table 3, for example), a limited investment in small -capacity, low-cost microcomputers might be the compromise which would most ameliorate this particular shortcoming.

Finally, the broad functional conclusion which materialised from the case study material is that comprehensive preparation for the computer-based society is most likely to emerge where, for whatever reasons, there is (a) an acknowledged school policy which recognises the importance of this relevant preparation for the future, (b) a body of teachers which is sufficiently dedicated to implementing this policy in a much broader context than computer studies alone, and (c) a minimum threshold of equipment which provides sufficient means for implementation.

The results of the case-study findings have indicated the extent to which schools in the sample are preparing pupils adequately for a society in which computers are 'commonplace and pervasive'. The sample was designed to be sufficiently heterogeneous to offer the possibilty of cross-sectioning schools on a national scale. Furthermore the LEA which offered the sample is generally recognised to be above average in its commitment to and provision for computer education.

In the light of these two conditions the authors feel that, despite the smallness of the sample, the results offer a guide to the overall situation. Hence the following conclusions emerge. Only 33 per cent of upper schools are offering anything like an adequate preparation for the society perceived in the above terms. Even with the best schools, the beneficiaries of this preparation are a minority of pupils, for example 20–37 per cent of their leavers. Deduced figures show that only 10 per cent of *all* leavers are adequately prepared, or, conversely, as many as 90 per cent of all leavers receive inadequate preparation. The figures indeed suggest that in the region of 50 per cent of *all* leavers have no meaningful interaction with computers. Finally, only about 17 per cent of upper schools (one in six) appear to be using microcomputers in the control function, despite its obvious industrial importance and the continuing topical discussion of relevance in education.

Furthermore, in the light of the figures derived in the last section an assessment of the general current need for training of further staff can be seen as something between 4 and 10 per cent of the teaching force, depending on the objectives of broad policy. Since both the schools used in the derivation of these figures give priority (though not exclusively) to computing examination courses and the direct vocational opportunities they afford, it is our conviction that if schools are to achieve a broad preparation reaching across the curriculum and the subject preferences of all pupils, that is (in a phrase), a preparation for living with computers, then 10 per cent is the more meaningful guide. In fact the dispersion of computer use on which this percentage is based is itself by no means ideal, indicating that the real need is probably a somewhat higher percentage.

The nature of the training is itself a critical consideration, and what is offered ought to venture beyond the immediate instrumental skills and enter the 'cultural' dimension of the influence of the 'pervasive computer'. Trained hands need adequate tools, and we have deduced that if the objectives of preparing all, or even a majority of, school-leavers for a computer-oriented society are to be met, the investment to be made in equipment remains substantial. In the case of schools currently providing no computer interaction for a large majority of their pupils, a limited investment in small-capacity, low-cost microcomputers might be the best solution.

As a final *caveat*, it is possible to interpret the details of government schemes as aiming to prime a greater number of pupils for further training for skilled jobs in microelectronics and computing, that is, preparing them for work rather than life generally in a society in which 'computers are commonplace and pervasive'. Important as this aspect is, we believe that living with computers is going to be the more rigorous test. The difference of emphasis we believe to be marginal in costs but significant in outlook. All pupils leaving the school gate for the last time are walking towards computers, not leaving them behind. Microcomputers in schools are therefore different from other teaching aids, making it imperative for teachers to acknowledge as much in shaping their attitude to school policy and its implementation.

References

Bennet, Y. (1980), 'Teachers' attitudes to curriculum innovation', *Vocational Aspect of Education*, XXXII, 83, December, pp. 71–6.

Bishop, L. K. (1967), 'Bureaucracy and the Adoption of Educational Innovation'. PhD dissertation, Claremont Graduate School. London: University Microfilm.

Chambliss, E. J. (1968), 'Attitudes of Teachers towards adopting Innovations and the Relationships of these Attitudes to other Variables'. PhD dissertation, Texas Technology College. London: University Microfilm.

Jenson, T. A. (1982), in R. Lewis and D. Tagg (eds.) (1982), *CAL: Scope, Progress and Limits*. Amsterdam: North Holland.

Rushby, J. (1979), *An Introduction to Computing*. London: Croon Helm.

Thorne, M. (1982), 'Information famine', *Times Educational Supplement*, No. 3427, 5 March, pp. 32.

5. CAL implementation

P. OPACIC and A. ROBERTS

Currently, in England and Wales, the most influential official organisation in the field of computer-assisted learning is the government-inspired Microelectronics Programme (MEP). In 1978 Labour proposed a programme with a budget of £12·5 million and a running time of five years. By 1979 the Conservatives had defeated Labour in the general election and the new government, after reviewing the programme, announced a reduced version in March 1980 having a budget of £8 million over a three-year period (1981–84). At that stage the general aim was to promote more and better software and materials for both teacher training and curriculum development. In November 1980, with the appointment of Richard Fothergill as director, MEP finally got off the ground, and in April 1981 a paper entitled *The Micro-electronics Education Programme (the Strategy)* (DES, 1981) was published, dealing with MEP's strategy and proposed aims.

The paper stated that the broad aim of MEP was 'to help schools to prepare children for life in a society in which devices and systems based on microelectronics are commonplace and pervasive'. The previous chapter reports the results of a investigation into microcomputer use in six upper schools. This one reviews teachers' responses to a questionnaire indicating the extent and the context of CAL implementation in the same schools. Before turning to these results, however, we scrutinise some of the strategic aims of CAL in schools and some of the factors which might impede their realisation.

For our purposes the main strategic aims of CAL are well stated by the MEP paper, and we shall use them as windows of expectation. Thus, in the context of technological and social change, the assumptions of the working model which underpin MEP strategy are:

1. Schools should be encouraged to respond to these changes by amending the content and approach of individual subjects in the curriculum and, in some cases, by developing new topics.
2. With the dual aim of enriching the study of individual subjects and of familiarising pupils with the use of the microcomputer itself, methods of teaching and learning should make use of the microcomputer and other equipment using microprocessors. This may be expected to add new and rewarding dimensions to the relationship between teacher and pupil.
3. Use should be made of the microcomputer to develop the individual pupil's capacity for independent learning and information retrieval (DES, 1981).

The new topics referred to above include micro-electronics in control technology; electronics and its applications in particular systems; computer studies; computer-aided design, data logging and data processing; word processing; information retrieval from data bases.

MEP also recognises the need to train teachers effectively to use CAL and related equipment, and it argues for several levels of training to meet different user needs, for example:

1. One to three-day courses aimed at improving awareness and familiarisation for teachers of subjects such as languages and the humanities (which seem far removed from electronics), and for careers teachers.
2. Specialist courses of up to a week's duration for teachers wishing to include new topics in their subject teaching.
3. Longer specialist courses of up to three months' duration covering, say, electronics for science and craft/design technology teachers and the skills for developing computer-based learning material in any subject. MEP has pump-primed a regional network of in-service training centres for the provision of such courses.

Finally, on the grounds that teacher access to information, advice and materials for teaching and learning is crucial, MEP is supportive of development at three levels: individual teachers in individual schools; local/regional project teams; national programmes. A network of information centres has been designed so that one centre serves seven or eight LEAs.

Resistance to CAL implementation

Enhancement of the curriculum and of the teaching and learning processes has been related, at least potentially, to the successful implementation of CAL in schools. Many educationalists contend, however, that there are philosophical and psychological barriers to be overcome before CAL can be effectively implemented. Thus Hennessy (1982) argues that in most secondary schools teachers' main priority is supervision, not teaching, and that such a priority is founded on the reality that the law requires young people to attend school up the age of sixteen but imposes no obligation to learn anything or to take part seriously in the learning process. As a consequence, teachers have evolved a preference for methods which minimise the potential for disruption by uninterested students. Of necessity, the preference provides the least amount of individual tuition, thereby allowing the teacher to give fullest attention to overall class supervision. In such circumstances any CAL methods which are expected 'to add new dimensions to relationships' and 'to develop independent learning' may well be regarded as incompatible with the overriding objective of supervisory control.

The next priority, according to Hennessy, is ensuring that students of some ability have the best chance of passing sixteen-plus examinations. The reasons he presents to support this assertion are that (a) one measure of teachers' abilities is how successful their students are in examinations, (b) students' academic future depends on satisfactory O and A level results. If immediate career prospects are added to academic future, it seems unlikely that a teacher will readily abandon a proven method of getting results in favour of an innovatory but untried alternative. And 'real world' parental concern for results could militate against the prospects of change and merge with a consensus which favours the *status quo*.

Furthermore, these extrinsic considerations may work in concert with intrinsic features of teacher psychology. Hence Burghes (1982) points to adults having a built-up resistence to new technology, which is sensed as being an intergral part of the younger person's world. It is commonplace, in the world of microprocessors, for students to have more knowledge of computers and computing than teachers. For the teacher whose claim to deference and respect in the teaching role relies on a 'font of knowledge' self-image, there is a risk of a dimminution in self-confidence if the font, in this particular context, is dry.

Recognition of the interactive nature of the learning process and its symbiosis with pliant and mobil relationships (rather than brittle and static ones) would be more consonant with the requisite meeting of minds. Problems of such relativities are equally applicable to the teacher and his older administrative seniors, and these can contribute significantly to the viscosity of the medium in which change has to take place.

In the worst case, where all these factors combine, we can appreciate that there would be formidable opposition to transcurricular implementation of CAL.

The study

The investigation was based on a sample of teachers from six upper schools chosen as a representative cross-section of an LEA's schools. The total staff in the six schools was approximately 390, and 25 per cent of this was accepted as the upper limit of a manageable sample size. The eventual number of teacher respondents totalled seventy-two (18·5 per cent). The overall response rate for the issued questionnaires was 87·5 per cent.

Having decided the sample size for each school, the next stage involved subdivision of the sample according to the broad curricular sectors (or departments) in the particular school. The transcurricular allocation of questionnaires was based on the number of teachers in each sector and was decided by discussion with a co-ordinator inside the school. The distribution of questionnaires itself had to be placed in the hands of the school co-ordinator with a request that (a) the distribution within each sector should try to reflect the age and the sex of the teachers in that sector, and (b) no teacher should receive more than one questionnaire (in case a teacher was working in two curricular sectors).

The questionnaire covered the areas of (a) use of CAL in classes, (b) sources of information which influenced interest in CAL, (c) potential users, (d) reasons for non-use of CAL, (e) subject areas which would benefit from the use of CAL, (f) contact with outside bodies, (g) parental interest. Space was provided for further comment at the end.

Results

The composition of the sample as a whole was approximately 33 per cent science teachers and 50 per cent male, which seems a broadly reasonable balance for two major elements of the sample. Some 13 per cent of all respondents were using CAL in their classes, 21 and 3 per cent for males and females respectively. The percentage of respondents acknowledging at least one source of possible CAL information was 47, and the female acknowledgment level was 35 per cent, compared with a male 58. Table 1 adds further detail to the general picture by determining the source acknowledgement rate per respondent, which averages out at 0·93, and at the same time widens the perspective by giving a discriminatory analysis of source referrals.

A reserve of potential users (among those who are currently non-users) was discovered which was 65 per cent overall, 55 per cent and 77 for female and male respondents respectively. In Table 2 we are looking for the constraints which hinder the application of this potential and as a result find that lack of equipment, expertise and time are all important in this respect. On average each non-user was hindered by 2·3 constraints (including 'Others').

One the basis that CAL might be encouraged by liaison with other interested parties outside the school, we examined the data and found that just 18 per cent of respondents had had some form of external contact. The list of external parties and the numbers of liaising respondents was as follows: university/college, four; local teachers' centre, three; another school, two; Schools Council industrial project (CRAC), one; Engineering Industry Training Board (COIC), one; Royal Sociey of Chemistry, one; private company, one.

Finally, 69 per cent of all respondents expressed an opinion on the question of parental interest, indicating that only a third thought that parents were interested in the use of CAL in schools.

Analysis and discussion of results

The respondent sample had a transcurricular composition of approximately 35 and 47 per cent of science and female teachers respectively, and seems to have had a broad balance between the various elements. The overall use of CAL was confined to only 13 per cent of respondents, although in schools IV and V the percentage rose to 20 and 27 respectively, reflecting the positive attitude of each school to the use of CAL. On policy, both schools gave the impression of being restrained by lack of equipment, and in fact school IV had made a policy decision to switch its resources to CAL in 1984. The sample of

Table 1 Extent of source[a] acknowledgement, including acknowledgement rate per respondent and relative frequency of acknowledgement

School[b]	MEP	Ed. per	Media	Social	Others	Total	Total respondents	Acknowl. per respondent
I	2	3	6	5	3	19	17	1·12
II	1	2	1	1	0	5	9	0·56
III	1	1	1	2	0	5	7	0·71
IV	1	2	2	5	2	12	15	0·80
V	1	2	4	5	5	17	15	1·13
VI	0	3	2	3	1	9	9	1·00
Total	6	13	16	21	11	67	72	0·93
Relative frequency (%)	9·0	19·4	23·9	31·3	16·4	100·0		

[a] Sources listed on questionnaire as: Microelectronics Programme (MEP); Educational periodicals (Ed. per.); Media, e.g. television; Social; Others.
[b] See note at end of chapter.

Table 2 Acknowledgement by non-users of reasons^a discouraging use of CAL, including rate per non-user and relative frequency of acknowledgement

School^b	Non-users	Lack of expertise	Lack of time	Lack of equipment	Other reasons	Total	Reasons per non-user
I	17	12	11	14	4	41	2·4
II	9	6	6	5	1	18	2·0
III	6	3	3	5	2	13	2·2
IV	12	8	7	9	6	30	2·5
V	11	7	6	10	5	28	2·5
VI	8	5	4	5	1	15	1·9
Totals	63	41	37	48	19	145	2·3
Relative frequency (%)		28·2	25·5	33·1	13·1	99·9	

^{a} The reasons shown in columns 3–6 were listed on the questionnaire.
^{b} See note at end of chapter.

male teachers in this school recorded a 38 per cent CAL usage rate.

On looking at the percentages of male and female respondents using CAL we found scores of 21 and 3 per cent for male and female teachers respectively (13 per cent overall) and a 'differential gradient' of 7/1, always in the same direction for all six schools. There seems therefore to be a significant difference in the exploitation of the possibilities of CAL, and to elucidate the point we tried to remove any science subject bias from the difference by analysing the data on a science/non-science base. The overall figures for science respondents showed that the male-female 'gradient' was reduced from 7/1 to 4/1, leaving the non-sciences with an increased gradient. This gave a more informed view of what was happening but still left us needing an explanation.

The analysis also highlighted the expected overall contrast between CAL use in science, at 24 per cent and non-science at 6·4 per cent, the latter being mainly 'subjects . . . where microelectronics applications may be less apparent' (DES, 1981). Presumably MEP short awareness-familiarisation courses for teachers of subjects such as languages and humanities and careers teachers will be aimed at lessening this contrast. In this context it may be necessary to see provisions for training and CAL implementation as a coherent whole in the planning process of in-service training.

We can now return to the sub-set of CAL users to see what type of software they were using in upper schools. In summary form this embraced the following: chemistry – class demonstration and individual work; commerce/economics – data processing and simulation; craft/design technology – quizzes, revision exercises and design using a light pen; geography – drill and practice and A level calculations using fieldwork data; mathematics – graphical work; physics – revision exercises. In the main the applications were of the simplest kind and there was no evidence of a break-out from the 'beachhead' subjects (those listed above). More optimistically, the small sample did in fact manage to exemplify all the paradigms defined by Kemmis et al. (1977): instructional – drill and practice; revelatory – simulation; conjectural – data processing; and emancipatory – computation of fieldwork data.

Even for science respondents the proportion of non-users among males and females was as high as 64 and 91 per cent respectively, leaving cavernous room for fulfilling the hope expressed in the foreward to the MEP paper (DES, 1981) that others might be encouraged to become involved in work being done in the subject areas.

The figures for school V science respondents demonstrated that locally comparable user rates for female and male respondents can emerge (33 and 40 per cent), but the smallness of the sample makes comparisons very sensitive to the slightest absolute change and reduces confidence in the figures.

In a further attempt to identify contributing factors to the difference between male and female respondents in CAL use we considered the possibility of a selective lack of information. In terms of access or referral to a minimum of one information source, only 47 per cent of all respondents qualified and the respective figures for male and female respondents are were 58 and 35 per cent. When we compared these figures with the user figures (viz. 13 per cent overall, 21 per cent for male and 3 per cent for female respondents), we gained an indicator of the importance of access to information sources and a measure of the overall resistence to the use of CAL. Thus the 'referral/user quotients' $58/21 = 2·8$ and $35/3 = 11·7$ yield an indicator measuring the relative extent of the barriers between information and implementation for male and female respondents.

When we further examined the question of source referral, by separating the data on the basis of science and non-science respondents, we found (a) almost equal percentage referral rates for female/science and female/non-science (36 and 35); and (b) a higher referral rate for male/non-science than for male/science (60 and 50 per cent). We have combined these data in order to compare referral and user rates (or percentages) on the basis of the referral/user quotient. This illustrates (a) a relatively close connection between source referral and CAL use for the male/science respondents (quotient 1·4); (b) a more attenuated connection for the female/science respondent (4·0); and (c) an attenuation similar to the latter for the male/non-science respondent (4·6). No analogous quotient for the female/non-science respondents is available, because there was no female user in this category. Using this quotient as a guide, the ranking of respondents in order of increasing apparent resistance to CAL implementation is male/science $<<$ female/science $<$ male/non-science $<<<$ female/non-science. (Note the heightened steps indicated by $<<$ and $<<<$.) Built-in resistance to new technology (Burghes, 1982) will be one element in the overall resistance to using CAL, even if the in-situ resistance owes more to conditioning than genetics. Thus the perceived resistance has a tendency to increase in the directions male to female and science to non-science, which conforms to orthodox stereotypical images of technological alienation.

In the case of CAL users we would expect the referral/user quotient to be unity, and this is the case for user/non-science respondents. However, for user/science respondents the quotient is only 0·67 as a result of two male respondents apparently implementing CAL spontaneously without reference to any knowledge source – a virgin birth of its kind!

If we compare schools on the basis of source acknowledgement per respondent in Table 1 and user rating we find that (a) school V has the highest score on either basis; and (b) school II has the lowest score on either basis. On the premise that a high source acknowledgement score is consonant with a generally more informed and motivated staff, then, other things being equal, this should correlate with the degree of CAL usage. Such is the case for the two extremes, schools V and II, but the middle rankings are not so clear-cut. For example, school I is ranked second on high acknowledgement score but equal bottom on CAL usage. The mediating facts are that, whilst the staff were interested in using CAL, they found themselves constrained by an under-resourced school of the inner-city, multi-racial type. In another case, school IV would be fourth ranked on CAL use by predication (based on its source acknowledgement) when in fact it actually ranked second. The higher ranking in this case was a direct result of the school's decision to commit its resources to CAL, and this change was under way.

If we now inspect Table 1 school by school to monitor the variation in the score for each acknowledged source it is consistently discernible that MEP is lowest or equal lowest scorer. Turning to the relative percentage frequencies in Table 1, we find that the order of decreasing acknowledgement frequency is: social > media > educational periodicals >> MEP. (Note the larger step down indicated by >>.)

In Table 3 we look at relative acknowledgement frequency in greater detail by analysing the data under the headings: science, non-science, male, female. In each of the four resulting categories we find that MEP is again consistently the lowest scorer. The summated rankings (a low score indicating a high acknowledgement frequency) confirm that as a source of information social is easily first, MEP easily last, and that educational periodicals and media are of almost equal

Table 3 Acknowledgement of sources by teachers: frequency percentages and rank order

	Social % Rank		Media % Rank		Ed. per % Rank		MEP % Rank	
Science/male	25	1	19	2=	19	2=	13	4
Science/female	33	1=	17	3=	33	1=	17	3=
Non-science/male	26	1	23	2=	23	2=	10	4
Non-science/female	50	1	36	2	7	3	0	4

middling importance. From the table we can deduce that (a) for science/female respondents social and educational periodicals are high-scoring sources; (b) for non-science/female respondents social (particularly) and media are high scorers.

We can add further that none of the six science CAL users and just one of the three non-science CAL users made reference to MEP, giving it percentage acknowledgement frequencies among the user category of 11 per cent, which compares with an overall 9 per cent for all respondents, and 0 and 33 per cent for science and non-science users. Combining the user data with the data in Table 3 we can further deduce MEP percentage acknowledgement frequencies among non-users for science and non-science respectively: $100 \times 3/(22 - 6) = 19$ per cent and $100 \times 2/(45 - 3) = 5$ per cent (with an overall value for non-users of $100 \times 5/(67 - 9) = 9$ per cent). Hence MEP achieves its higher scores as an information source with non-science users (33 per cent) and science non-users (19 per cent).

Although specificity increases as we move from social, media and periodicals as sources to MEP as a source, which would contribute to a lower acknowledgement rate, we might nevertheless expect MEP to emerge much more favourably, particularly in view of the emphasis it places on: keeping teachers informed; providing access to information and advice; setting up a network of information centres; and pump-priming regional in-service training centres (DES, 1981).

The following quotations are taken from respondents' comments and relate to the above MEP aims and objectives: (a) 'Advice in subject areas other than obvious ones related to CAL seems very difficult to come by'; (b) 'Never seen any information'; (c) More information could be forthcoming as to how CAL can be used'; (d) 'We would like to be shown programs available'; (e) 'Any chance of introducing teachers to use of computers in education?'; (f) 'It would be useful to be able to get first-hand experience of computers and suitable software'; (g) 'Would appreciate opportunity to learn guidelines – perhaps a course of some description'; (h) 'I believe it would be a great help if elementary courses in computing could be organised for simple souls like me'. The sum of all the evidence seems to suggest the need for more interaction between practioners and MEP agencies or centres.

Under the source heading 'Others', one respondent mentioned the Schools Council chemistry series, another the Schools Council industry project and one respondent listed careers service, teachers' centre and in-service training. (If these sources were regarded as MEP-linked and the three respondents consequently allocated to MEP, its overall acknowledgement frequency would increase from 9·0 to 13·4 per cent, which is still below educational periodicals.) Other respondents referred to: school policy and resource acquisition, college, Open University, Royal Society of Chemistry, university diploma course, home use of computer and 'my own child'.

In view of the large non-user population (79 and 97 per cent for male and female respondents respectively) it would be interesting to know what proportion would like to use CAL. These potential users are a substantial latent resource of 77 and 55 per cent for male and female respondents respectively and 65 per cent overall. The gradient of the sex differential is consistent for all schools except school III, which happens to be an all-girl school. This school also had the highest proportion of potential female users (75 per cent), and school I, which was deliberately committing resources to CAL, had the next highest (71 per cent). There was significant variation in the observed female potential, whereas male potential was consistently high. We have no details to explain this variance for females.

The dissection of potential users into the sub-categories revealed that (a) the male-female differential persists across the science/non-science boundary, becoming more emphatic in the process (male/female quotients: $78/60 = 1·30$ and $76/52 = 1·46$); (b) the high male potential hardly changes across this boundary; and (c) the female potential decreases in the non-science category from 60 per cent to almost 50. Therefore in terms of a possible selective programme of information dissemination and encouragement these two female percentages outline the size of the main targets.

With such generally high user potential among current non-users it would be useful to learn something of the barriers which nevertheless impede CAL application. Table 2 displays the information gleaned by the survey, and we conclude that the barriers are formidable when on average there are 2·3 reasons for not using CAL. (There is insufficient information to offer an explanation of the variation from 1·9 to 2·5 for different schools.) Lack of expertise, time and equipment are all important, the latter most of all. When the information is broken down into more coherent categories it shows that (a) for male science, male non-science and female science respondents, lack of equipment is the most important reason; (b) for female non-science respondents lack of expertise is top of the list. It is interesting to note that lack of expertise diminishes in importance in the order: female non-science, male non-science, female science, and male science (44 per cent). Consequently, in terms of training, female non-science teachers would benefit most of all from the short familiar/awareness courses proposed by MEP as one of its objectives. Whether this group is regarded as a priority target depends on other things – policy, for example. Thus there is still a 44–60 per cent shortfall in expertise in the science sector and the evidence suggests that the subsequent implementation rate would be higher for this group, which could justify a higher planning priority. The problem of lack of equipment and time is a broader question of resource availability and allocation.

Other reasons for non-use of CAL were specifically indicated by some respondents: (a) lack of need/interest (five respondents): modern languages, art/design, English, science (none of these indicated equipment, time or expertise as a reason); (b) lack of software (seven): modern languages, science, physics, mathematics, history; (c) lack of information/advice (four): humanities, mathemtics, biology, art/design; (d) lack of relevance to subject/syllabus (two): PE, music/history; (e) classes too large (one): chemistry. Just about every one of these, given good will, would have benefited from knowledge of and contact with MEP and its agencies.

In the 'Results' section we identified the external institutions with which 18 per cent of all respondents had some form of liaison. The majority of liaisons are local ones undertaken by individual teachers, 50 per cent of whom are CAL users, without the benefit of a coherent network of collaborative interactions and cross-fertilisations which is a typical MEP specification. The general image conveyed by the survey is of teachers isolated, in the main, from the development work taking place in MEP agencies, with no obvious means of discovering what is happening. An effective self-help strategem is for a school to commit itself to CAL and to make a collective effort to accommodate it, which is what one of the six schools in the survey did by dropping computer studies and initiating its own development of hardware resources, staff training programmes, links with publishers and co-operation with the LEA computer division. Given sufficient consensus within the school, this seems a sensible way to approach CAL implementation, particularly if individual teachers are pointed (if necessary) in the direction of sources and encouraged to move forward to implementation. The dropping of computer studies entirely as a curricular option is a more controversial issue, giving rise to some adverse comments from students and parents which are in alignment with the expectations of Hennessy (1982) that we alluded to earlier. Thus in the words of one respondent, 'Parents show strong interest in Computer Studies and regard the shift in use of computer resources to CAL as a denial of access to specific subject qualifications.' This neatly encapsulates the dilemma which limited resources force on schools, because computer skills related to job prospects are generally of greater concern to parents than CAL. Thus the estimate of parental interest in CAL, which was reported in the 'Results' section as 33 per cent, has to be regarded with caution, especially as some of the respondents' comments seemed to be referring to computers generally rather than CAL specifically.

Although teaching in conventional ways, 65 per cent of the sixty-three non-users indicated subject areas which in their opinion would have benefited from CAL. Most of this software relates to the simple instructional and revelatory paradigms of Kemmis et al. (1977) and is therefore most probably already available from commercial and LEA sources. The nominated subject areas are as follows. Chemistry: formulae and equations; general calculations; solubilities; rates of reactions and graphical representation. Careers: business games; careers information, updating and 'research'; matching skills to the job; 'diagnostic aspects generally'. Craft/design technology; graphics, design methodology of the interactive kind (allowing for iteration and modification of the original idea); generally more interactive software. English: development of individual skills such as spelling, vocabulary, punctuation, syntax, interpreting table and diagrams; individual learning packages for both slow and gifted students; decision-making exercises; 'character/relationships/role assessment (analysis) in conjunction with video facilities (aimed to improve student expression)'; group learning tasks. English as second language: individual spelling, puncuation and vocabulary practice for slow learners; comprehension and sentence structure work (with the additional aim of 'giving them some sense of involvement with the technology of the age'); interactive cloze procedure. Geography: statistical analysis of fieldwork and other data; 'spatial awareness in economic geography'; various geographical models, e.g. Weber, Christaller, Von Thuness. History: analysis of census returns and population figures; graphical and statistical presentation; data base packages; games showing cause and effect; simulation exercises generally. Home economics: food analysis. Mathematics: basic mathematics practice; algebraic substitution; statistical representation; graphs of functions; interactive motion geometry graphical work and statistics. Modern languages: self-paced programmed learning; 'storing work sheets'; self-correcting drills with built-in gradients of difficulty; comprehension exercises; many grammatical areas (French verbs, German word order, adjective endings). Music: 'serial and stochastic techniques of composition'; computerised synthesiser; ready-made packages. Physics: simulation of experiments; interfacing experiments; electronic circuits. Special education: numeracy and language development software.

The topics clearly illustrate that non-users have an appreciation of the possibilities of CAL, and this supports the argument that it is the translation of appreciation into classroom implementation that is the main problem, pointing again to the need to integrate training with plans for implemenation. The reasons for lack of implementation are many and complex; lack of expertise, time and equipment are only three of the more prominent ones, and built-in resistance (inherent or conditioned) to new technology has already been mentioned and related to the work of Burghes (1982).

Non-users are not isolated from the frustrations which users have to cope with, such as incompatibility between different machines and the lack of suitable rooms, technical back-up, software and micronetting. Even with appropriate software there may still be problems. 'Two years ago,' writes one respondent, 'I spent a lot of time preparing work based on the Schools Council's *Sulphuric acid* software package. It was good, and the pupils enjoyed it, working after school. But if I were to repeat the exercise I would want ten machines with central loading. The time involved in getting to know a program is also quite considerable (several hours when work sheets are to be prepared) and at present I would find great difficulty in making time available.' A biology teacher commented on the difficulty of fitting CAL into a lesson with access to just one microcomputer and another teacher pointed out that large classes do not help.

Comments on software quality also have a sustained drift round the staff room and include such expressions as: software is often designed round the computer rather than the teaching objective (physics); commercial software fails to hit the nail on the head (chemistry); sophisticated software for individual study is not available (modern languages); available software in CDT is shallow and uninspired and design work requires iterative interaction and change of scale and projection which mean complex (and expensive) programs; much of the available biology software is poor, my own programming skills are not strong and the topics can be taught better in other ways; there is little suitable material for English as a second language, a limited range for remedial language teaching in the thirteen-plus range and nothing specifically on sentence structures. MEP and software agencies clearly have much to do to gain the confidence of practioners. To quote a teacher of physics, 'Experience of programs in earlier days has discouraged me from using them.' The final summation of the predicament of good software design comes from a female teacher of Mathematics: '. . . it needs not only good programmers and subject specialists but also specialists in the psychology of learning, that is teachers'.

Conclusions

Accepting that the respondents from a cross-section of upper schools in a well informed and forward planning LEA are broadly typical of the general scene, the results of the case study show that, despite all the earnest public discussion of CAL, the extent of its implementation in schools is limited to only 13 per cent of all teachers. Male teachers, as might be expected on the basis of the science bias referred to earlier, register a higher participation rate of 21 per cent, as against 3 per cent for female teachers. Likewise, science subjects in general have a more extensive network of practioners (24 per cent) than non-science subjects (6·4 per cent). Presumably either the 'Heineken effect' of MEP has not yet been fully established or these trends represent the current 'natural order of things'.

The evidence from the pattern of CAL usage shows that generally we are still at the relatively simple instructional and revelatory modes of CAL use (in the majority of cases there is failure to engage in CAL in any way at all) and there is little evidence of the genesis of the new topics listed by DES (1981). This is not to deny that good work is going on, for we are aware of exceptions which have not fallen within the sample; it is simply a reflection of the general stage of development as we have tested it. When non-use is as high as 91 per cent (science/ female) or even as low as 64 per cent (science/male) there is, as expressly desired by the DES, room enough for others to get involved in established activities.

In terms of acknowledging a minimum of one source of information on CAL, only 47 per cent of all teachers satisfy the requirement, although the male rate (58 per cent) is higher than the female rate (35 per cent) and may be, in part, the cause of the differential CAL implementation rate. Other evidence, however, suggests that the advance to implementation is the critical phase and the degree of difficulty in achieving it depends on the sex and subject type. Thus, with overall source referral/CAL user quotients of 2·8 and 11·7 respectively, male teachers seem to experience less severe impedance than female teachers. On the other hand, sub-category quotients indicate that there is an order of increasing impedance of the kind: male/science, female/science, male/non-science and female/non-science. This directionality is in broad alignment with conventional stereotypes which have some basis in past fact.

When measuring schools by the number of sources of information acknowledged per member of (respondent) staff and the percentage of (respondent) staff involved in the use of CAL, we find a positive connection between these two parameters only at the extremes. In the middle range we have to know the schools' attitudinal and resource profiles in order to make a fit.

When we examine the relative importance of sources, as determined by their acknowledgement by respondents, we find a diminishing overall order from social to media and educational periodicals to MEP. More refined details in this analysis show that social and educational periodicals are the most important sources for the science/female category, whilst social (very particularly) and media are the high scorers for non-science/female.

Admittedly MEP is a more closely defined reference target than 'social' and 'media', for example, and, therefore may be less regulary hit. We have presented arguments, however, which allow for this, and our opinion is that MEP finishes with a profile which is much lower than it should be, given the statement of its strategy, aims and objectives. The inclusion of unedited quotes has exemplified the point.

There is obviously a large non-user population, and interrogation of this sector has revealed a large pool of potential users measuring 65 per cent overall and 77 and 55 per cent for male and female categories. This male/female differential applies to all schools except one and to both science and non-science categories. The data on sub-categories indicate that female teachers, whether science or non-science, are the prime target for any selective programme of 'education' in the use of CAL.

Barriers to CAL implementation have been assessed and, in terms of just one of these, namely lack of expertise, the order of increasing importance is science/male then female and finally non-science/male then female. This knowledge might act as a more concise guide to the organisation of training, and we make the point that to be effective this training ought to be integrated with post-training plans to implement CAL. Supporting evidence for this is the application awareness of so many non-users.

Among the respondents 18 per cent liaise with outside institutions and 50 per cent of these are CAL users. There is a chicken-and-egg question here but, in general, the benefits of this involvement cannot be doubted even when it is much more of an individual pursuit than a collaborative MEP activity.

One school, deliberately implementing CAL at the expense of computer studies, has predictably encountered the legitimate concern of parents and students, thus illustrating the *Catch 22* situation which characterises so many educational decisions in the context of limited resources.

Finally, some well established opinions of available software and some experiences of the educational use of microcomputers have been rehearsed, ending with a quote defining the need for the synthesis of multidisciplinary skills in the design of educationally effective programs.

We started this chapter with the benefit of the expectations which we deliberately chose to perceive in the MEP statement (DES, 1981). These expectations embraced: changes in education content, processes, interactions and horizons; a spectrum of training opportunities from introductory to programming skills within a network of training centre; and wide ranging access to information, advice materials via regional information centres. The case study findings neither magnify nor belittle these perceived expectations but rather present a 'bespoke' measurement of their current shape for a sample of the teaching fabric.

Note

The two studies reported in chapters 4 and 5 were separated by more than a year. The internal characteristics of the schools change quite quickly. For example, the spread of CAL waxes and wanes with staff appointments and resignations and with policy changes. School IV made a decision to concentrate on CAL and to drop computer studies. As a result of such changes the 'identities' of schools have drifted with time and this movement has not been comprehensively monitored.

References

Burghes, D. (1982), 'In-service micro courses for the teaching profession', in I. C. H. Smith (ed.), *Microcomputers in Education*. Chichester: Ellis Horwood.

Hennessy, K. (1982), 'A systems approach to curriculum development, the Manchester project for computer studies in schools', in C. Smith (ed.), *Microcomputers in Education*. Chichester: Ellis Horwood.

Kemmis, S., Atkin, R., and Wright, E. (1977), *How do Students Learn?* Occasional Paper No. 5., Centre of Applied Research in Education, University of East Anglia.

Department of Education and Science (1981), *The Micro-electronics Programme (The Strategy)*. London: HMSO.

6. Evaluating software for the classroom

DAVID G. REAY

Innovations in education are notoriously slow to take root. Often only a few teachers are involved in early development work. The dissemination which follows a successful preliminary stage is frequently small-scale and achieved through networks of teachers with similar classroom needs. Only gradually, as an increasing number of teachers become aware of them and try them out, do new ideas become incorporated into general classroom practice. The pace with which microelectronics in general and the use of computers in particular have been introduced into education has, by comparison, been uncharacteristically and breathtakingly rapid. There is no evidence here of the often quoted fifteen-year time lag between introduction and widespread appearance in schools. Large sums of government money have been spent on the development and provision of hardware and software, with the result that every school in the country should have at least one computer of its own. Many schools will have networks of computers linking classrooms and schools, both within and beyond the British Isles, and more will be joining them as the decade progresses. National bodies have been set up to co-ordinate training and development work, and there is growing pressure on teachers to incorporate microelectronics into every area of the curriculum.

The pace has been so rapid that teachers are faced with large numbers of programmes (software) but are likely to have received little or no training or guidance in their selection and use. Increased in-service training is going some way towards alleviating the problems of teachers who wish to make the best use of micros, but retraining is a slow process. It will be several years, at least, before the majority of teachers have attended appropriate courses.

Futhermore, there is a dearth of soundly designed research-based evaluation studies of the educational use of microcomputers from which teachers can obtain guidance in deciding when, how and indeed whether to use micros in their teaching. Although it is only through extensive research that a body of generalisable knowledge can be built up, it would be unrealistic to expect every computer program to be the subject of controlled research before it was used by teachers.

The selection of software is, and because of the dynamic nature of microelectronics will continue to be, a problem facing all teachers using computers in their classrooms. Program advertising gives some guidance, but information is frequently based on imagined claims rather than confirmed evidence. Often the questions teachers would like to have answered are not addressed. There appears to be a need, therefore, for an approach to evaluating software which is general enough to be widely applicable but specific enough to provide the kind of information that will allow decisions to be made about the acceptability of programs under consideration. This is a need which has been expressed by many teachers the writer has worked with.

During the last three years the writer has worked with teachers in the USA and England on the development of such an approach to the assessment of software for educational use. It involves treating microcomputer software as one more educational tool which must satisfy sound instructional principles in order to be acceptable in the classroom, not become accepted simply because it is *The* new technology. There is a danger of the latter occurring; one of the claims frequently made for the use of computers in schools is that children of today will live in a world of computers. However, only a very small proportion of the present school population is likely to encounter microcomputers in anything other than a user's role. One does not need to be able to programme a computer to operate a micro-controlled washing machine or Prestel receiver, any more than it is necessary to be knowledgeable about the inner workings of an internal combustion engine to be able to drive a car. Computer designers go out of their way to disguise the electronic contents of micro-controlled equipment and make it easy to operate by non-experts. Because of this it is the writer's view that the use of microcomputers and their attendant software in schools must be justified in broad educational terms. 'Does the use of computer software help us to achieve our aims in terms of child learning?' 'Does its use improve the efficiency of teaching in terms of child learning?' 'Is what is being learned of value?' are some of the questions which must be addressed. Implicit in this kind of approach is the need for a clear idea of our aims.

The remainder of the chapter consists of a checklist for evaluating software. It is the outcome of several years' use by teachers in primary and secondary schools in the USA and England. Designed for use by individual teachers, or groups of teachers involved in the selection of software, it is intended as a means of focusing attention on the kinds of question one could usefully ask before using a particular piece of software with a group of children or a whole class. The version described here has been much refined as a result of comments made by teachers who used the original. The checklist is not designed to be exhaustive but, by directing attention to key issues, to act as a guide to the selection of software.

The checklist focuses on two main aspects of program use: (a) *management* and (b) *educational content*. It has been found that for maximum effectiveness a two-stage approach should be used. (1) The first stage should be carried out by the teacher(s) working through the program documentation and the program itself. (2) The second should involve the teacher(s) watching one or at most two children of appropriate age or stage of learning, using the program under classroom conditions.

The main questions are italicised, and followed by either subsidiary questions or comments. It will be necessary to read the comments only once, so use of the checklist will not be as arduous as a first glance might suggest.

Stage 1

Section A, Management
1 *Is the program available on disc, tape, EPROM or all three?*

(a) If the program is on disc, is the kind of disc drive specified? For example, BBC disc drives can be either forty-track or eighty-track – a program recorded on a forty-track disc will not operate if used with an eighty-track disc drive, and vice versa.

(b) If available on EPROM (pre-recorded 'chip' which must be inserted into the spaces provided inside the computer case) is there space for it in your computer? If you have more than three programs on EPROM you should obtain an expansion board which will allow up to twelve EPROMs to be used. There are advantages for school use in having programs on EPROMs, including ease of operation and the difficulty of erasing them (they have to be subjected to lengthy periods of ultraviolet light), but repeatedly inserting and removing an EPROM is not be recommended. Once in place it should remain in place.

2 *Are any ancillary pieces of hardware necessary (e.g. a printer)?*
   (a) Is the ancillary equipment available?
   (b) If not, is the effectiveness of the programme likely to be reduced?

3 *Is a user's guide provided?* (If not, go to 7.)

4 *If provided, is the user's guide*

   (a) Easy to read?
   (b) Easy to access information? (Does it have a contents, index etc.?)

5 *Does the user's guide include the following information?* (If not, you will have to load the program into your computer and run it to determine the answer.)

   (a) An overview of the program, including a statement of what kind of program it claims to be, e.g. drill and practice, concept teaching, and so on. (Write this down; you will use the information later.)
   (b) A statement of the learning objective.
   (c) A description of program operation and how to handle problems which may arise.
   (d) A statement of any prerequisite skills or knowledge.
   (e) A 'diagnostic' pre-measure (to determine whether children would benefit from using the programme – they may already know, or be sufficiently well-practiced in its content).
   (f) Some form of checking whether the user learns anything as a result of using the program. (If this is not present you may have to design your own material to find out whether the program does in fact achieve the claims for it.)
   (g) Details of any other materials required.
   (h) Any difficulties which may occur when making a work copy of the original program?

To answer these questions you will have to try out the program – choose somewhere quiet and a time when you are unlikely to be disturbed.

6 *Are the operating procedures consistent throughout?* For example, is the way in which the program 'knows' information has been entered from the keyboard the same throughout? Ideally it should be. (Having to press RETURN after some key presses but not after others is not uncommon. Not only is it frustrating for the user but it tends to divert attention away from the learning content of the program and towards the operation of the machine.)

7 *Is sufficient information to operate the program provided on screen?*

8 *If not, is written material provided which provides the guidance necessary?* If such a guide is provided:
(a) Can the intended audience read and understand it? (You'll have to give it to a member of the intended audience to find out accurately)
(b) Is the guide sufficiently detailed?

9 *To what extent is the program under user control?* For example, can the user change their input *before* the program acts on it? (Good programs will allow this.)

Section B, Educational aspects of the program

11 *What kind of program does it claim to be?* (You have notes on this from Stage 1, section 5(a).

12 *What kind of program is it?* (The two things are not always the same.)

13 *Is what the program claims to teach* (e.g. problem-solving, calculating area, punctuation) *worth teaching?*

14 *Does the approach fit in with your aims?* Specify in detail and in writing. (If it does not, it may not be worth while going any further!)

15 *Does the content fit in with the learning objectives for your class?* Specify in detail and in writing.

16 *Can the teaching or practice which the program claims to provide be achieved more efficiently through a more traditional approach* (e.g. teaching left and right by having children walk around obstacles rather than guiding a cartoon figure round an on-screen maze)?

17 *Is the program concerned with:*

    (a)   Concept learning? See section C below.
    (b)   Rule learning? See section D below.
    (c)   Memory training? See section E below.
    (d)   Problem solving? See section F below.
    (e)   Practice? See section G below.

Section C, If concept learning

18 *Most or all of the following elements should be present – are they?*

    (a)   A definition or statement identifying the critical attributes (e.g. the critical attributes of a square).
    (b)   'Matching' exercises involving examples and non-examples.
    (c)   'Attribute isolation' – the use of attention-focusing devices, e.g. colour sectional drawings, etc., which isolate critical attributes.
    (d)   'Contrast practice' (magnified or exaggerated differences).
    (e)   Single discriminations before mixed up.
    (f)   Examples tied to learners' past experience.
    (g)   Gradual reduction in the scale of differences between examples?
    (h)   To show that the concept has been learned, are novel unencountered instances used as tests?

Section D, If rule learning

19 *All or most of the following should be in evidence – are they?*

    (a)   The performance expected of the learner?
    (b)   Presentation of the rule?
    (c)   Provision of examples?
    (d)   Opportunities for practice?
    (e)   Ample and appropriate feedback?
    (f)   Opportunity for the learner to demonstrate acquisition of the rule?
    (g)   Integrated review of the rule?

Section E, If memory training

20 *The following should be present – are they?*

    (a)   Does the content mean anything to the intended audience?
    (b)   Is repetition used?

(c) Is the repetition appropriate?
(d) Is the organisation of the content clear to the learner?
(e) Do related items appear close to each other in time and/or space?
(f) Are the number of new items presented in range 5 ($\pm$ 2)?
(g) Will the consequences of learning be of meaning to the learner?
(h) Are *all* correct responses reinforced during the early stages?
(i) There should be *no* negative feedback in the early stages (and why have any later?)

Section F, If problem-solving
21 *The following should be present – are they?*

(a) A clear description of the pre-knowledge required – in terms of processes understood rather than procedures learned.
(b) Information to the learner about what is to be achieved?
(c) Instructions which encourage the learner to discover a solution him/herself? (Directions should not detail the steps to a solution.)
(d) Instructions which stimulate recall of relevant rules or methods of solution?

Section G, If practice
22 *Ask the following questions:*

(a) Has the subject matter which is to be practised already been taught?
(b) Have the children reached the point of requiring practice?
(c) Is the nature of the practice appropriate to the content taught?
(d) Is the feedback positive?
(e) Is revision teaching included in the program?
(f) Is a performance record provided which gives diagnostic information?
(g) Is interference introduced (e.g. timed tasks when you want the children to practise in their own time)?

When you have completed this section you will be in a position to decide whether the programme looks promising or whether it simply does not fit the needs of your class. If the latter you should go no further. If it looks reasonable, move to Stage 2.

Stage 2

To be carried out with one or at most two children. The children should be members of the group which will use the program if it is selected. You should *observe* how the children use the program. The aim of this exercise is to identify the kind of problems children are likely to have if you decide to use the program in your classroom. You may find that a program which claims to be easy to use is not but that with appropriate teaching it could be useful. This part of the process will help you identify where and what kind of teaching is required. Make notes on any difficulties demonstrated by the children and provide guidance only as a last resort.

1 *Can the child read and understand any documentation which is essential for easy use of the program?*
2 *Can the child start the program without assistance?*
3 *Is it clear to the child what he/she is expected to do throughout the program?*
4 *Can the child operate the program easily with the information provided* (either on-screen or in the documentation)?
5 *Can the child access on-screen instructions from any point in the program?* (This is a valuable feature, especially in long and complex programs.)
6 *Does the program introduce interference* (e.g. the child has to pay more attention to how to operate the program at the cost of attention to its content)?
7 *Does the program capture and hold attention?* There is danger in judging the value of a program simply on its ability to motivate children to pay attention. Although there is a shortage of research findings its does appear that computers are intrinsically attention-grabbing instruments no matter what the quality of the software may be. However, if the child has no inclination to continue with a program after a short exposure to it, its value becomes questionable.
8 *Can the child operate the program the way he/she would prefer?* This will include: (a) the pace of presentation, (b) repetition of instructions, (c) the level of difficulty. One of the benefits claimed for computer software is that it can be written to accommodate a variety of learning styles. Does the program under review allow this?

9. *Is the organisation of the content obvious to the child?* (it helps if it is).

The final stage

By the time you reach this point you will have a fairly comprehensive picture of the software under review, its management strengths and weakness and some child reactions to it. The next step is the difficult one. Using this information and any other impressions collected during the investigation, the decision to use or not to use must be made. Evaluation supplies the information for decision-makers but cannot make the decisions. It falls to the individual or group of teachers to decide that a program should or should not be used, or what changes or additions are necessary to improve its effectiveness: it may be decided to carry out a small action research study to determine the degree to which the learning improvement which is claimed actually occurs, or to incorporate a demonstration or teaching approach which is not part of the program's specification.

Whatever is decided, this checklist can only inform. The teachers who were involved in its development felt that the checklist helped them focus attention on aspects of a program they might otherwise have missed. They also felt that it provided them with the basis for developing a personal set of criteria against which to evaluate the use of computers in their classrooms.

Computers are here, and provide educational opportunities previously undreamed of. Only if software and hardware can meet serious educational criteria will computers avoid joining other technological innovations, like programmed learning machines, in gathering dust at the back of the highest shelf in the school stock-cupboard.

References

Briggs, L. J. (ed.) (1977), *Instructional Design: Principles and Applications*. Englewood Cliffs: Educational Technology Publications.

Fleming, M. and Levie, W. H. (1978), *Instructional Message Design: Principles from the Behavioural Sciences*. Englewood Cliffs: Educational Technology Publications.

Gale, L. E., and Gottfredson, C. (1982), 'Criteria for Designing Instruction: An Abbreviated Checklist, paper presented to The Eighth Annual SIETAR Conference, Long Beach, California, March.

Webster, W. J. (1976), The Evaluation of Instructional Materials', Association for Educational Communications and Technology, October.

7. Evaluating CAL in the classroom

JOHN L. CHATTERTON

This chapter outlines the changes that occur in the science classroom when computer-assisted learning techniques are used. Lesson observations in a range of schools, using *A Systematic Classroom Analysis Notation*, SCAN, has shown that the use of CAL can produce a qualitative improvement in the learning environment. These changes are most marked when CAL-based lessons are compared with 'normal' theory lessons – in the great majority of cases CAL was used as an alternative approach to what would otherwise have been a 'theory' lesson. There were, however, many apparent similarities between CAL-based lessons and 'practical' lessons, in terms both of lesson structure and of teacher and pupil behaviour.

Classroom observation

SCAN had been described in detail elsewhere (Beeby *et al.*, 1979), but a brief description of its operation is necessary if the results outlined below are to be understood. Basically, it is a form of shorthand which allows the observer to record what happens in a lesson on three time scales, simultaneously. These 'time scales' are referred to as 'Activity', 'Episode' and 'Event' levels. During the observation a detailed record is built up within each time scale, giving a clear picture of classroom behaviour and management. The most detailed observations are at the 'Event' level (the shortest time scale). For example, questions are classified on two three-point scales: the *depth of demand* made by the question:

α   The recall of a single fact or act.

β The connection of several facts or acts (a pupil may be asked to describe what was seen in an experiment or to list the physical properties of covalent compounds).

γ And extension of previous skill or understanding (this may involve fitting experimental data to an existing pattern or generating a 'new' pattern from the data).

and the *level of guidance* given:

1 Maximum guidance: a highly structured situation in which the pupil recognises that a choice must be made from a restricted number of alternatives.

2 A more open situation in which connection, rather than simple selection, is required.

3 Minimum guidance: an open-ended situation in which the pupil must choose from a wide range of alternatives, synthesise data and ideas, etc. The situation is left as open as possible.

An examination of the SCAN-records of lessons has revealed differences in the lesson structures, not only for different teacher/class combinations but also for the same combination in differing settings, and it is the use of SCAN in this latter situation which has proved especially useful in assessing the changes introduced by the use of CAL.

To illustrate the types of change which have been found to occur, this chapter considers the work of four typical teachers.

Changes at the Activity level

One striking change in lesson structure becomes apparent if the proportion of time spent in individual and small-group work is compared for those lessons involving some use of CAL with the more traditional lesson styles (for convenience referred to as 'theory' and 'practical' lessons). Table 1 compares the percentage of time devoted to individual or small group work in a series of lessons given by the four teachers.

When 'CAL' lessons are compared with 'Theory' lessons, the increase in time spent in individual or small-group work seems to support the view that the computer can relieve the teacher of the role of task-setter and allow him/her to move round the class in a supportive role – giving advice and help, prompting new ideas and

Table 1 Percentage of time in individual or small-group work

Teacher	CAL in use	'Theory' lesson	'Practical' lesson
1	75	20	63
2	73	26	–
3	31	0	47
4	55	3	36

checking the understanding of established concepts. Practical lessons also show a higher percentage of time spent in individual or small-group work, possibly for similar reasons – once the practical task has been explained the teacher is, again, freed from the role of task-setter.

There is also a significant change in the type of activity taking place in the three types of lesson. Task-related pupil-pupil dialogue was virtually absent in the 'theory' lessons, whereas it played a significant part in both 'CAL' and 'practical' lessons.

This, again, is seen as a result of the changed structure of the lesson and as indicative of a move away from a traditional teacher-centred approach towards a more informal pupil-centred structure.

Changes at the Episode level

Differences are also apparent at the Episode level, where the SCAN records show a greater number of (shorter) episodes in lessons involving CAL or practical work. Table 2 shows the average length of episodes (in minutes) for the same series of lessons used for the previous table. This increase in the number of episodes, in lessons involving CAL, reflects the differences in the structure of these lessons compared with the traditional 'theory' lesson. Both the increase in small-group work and the alleviation of the role of 'task-setter' encourage the teacher to move from one group to another, discussing specific problems and strategies with each individual or group. This style of teaching will become increasingly

Table 2 Average length of episodes (minutes)

Teacher	CAL in use	'Theory' lesson	'Practical' lesson
1	1·9	3·0	1·6
2	3·3	5·0	–
3	1·8	2·8	2·6
4	2·5	3·0	3·3

important as, with the falling school roll, a wider range of ability is likely to be found in a given class or set.

The nature of the episodes themselves is also changed: for example, the number of teacher-based 'explaining' and 'initiating' episodes is reduced, while the number of episodes of 'coaching' (teacher working with an individual or small group of pupils) and, within a group of pupils, of 'arguing' or 'searching' (for a pattern or answer) is increased. Indeed, the SCAN records show that, for small-group work activities in lessons involving CAL, 'coaching' forms the basis of the great majority of teacher-initiated episodes.

Changes at the Event level

Changes also occur at the most detailed level recorded in SCAN – the event or remark level. Table 3 shows the proportion of some different question types used by one teacher, with a third-year middle-band chemistry group for lessons with and without the use of CAL. The figures in Table 3 are fairly typical of the lessons observed and suggest that, when CAL is used, the depth of demand of questions tends to increase (shown by the greater proportion of β questions) and the questions become more open (shown by the greater proportion of Guidance Level 2 questions). It would seem, therefore, that the use of CAL can encourage constructive changes at both tactical and strategic levels in lesson organisation and management.

Differences are also apparent between the pupil–pupil dialogue occurring in CAL sessions and that in practical sessions. In 'practical' work the pupils tend to concentrate on the details of the experiment, with remarks such as 'What temperature do we use?' 'How much do we add?' or 'Stir it up' far outnumbering questions about the causes of the changes observed or the reasons for a particular procedure. While the simple type of dialogue is also present when CAL is used, there is an increased tendency to discuss such things as 'What happens if we increase the temperature?' or 'Why has the yield gone

Table 3 *Differences in question types*

	Ratio of question types	
	Depth of demand $\alpha : \beta$	Level of guidance 1 : 2
CAL used	1 : 0·9	1 : 1·4
CAL not used	1 : 0·3	1 : 0·5

down?'. The pupils are led to question the reasons behind the 'facts' generated by the computer model and to develop a 'feel' for the principles involved. The fact that this type of dialogue is encouraged, or at least allowed, means that pupils are able to vocalise their ideas about the topic and to subject them to comment by their friends, without the stress which may accompany presenting the ideas to the whole class. Consequently, hypotheses tend to be suggested and discarded (or accepted) much more readily within the small group, than is usually the case when the discussion takes place before the whole class. The increased security of the small-group environment may be an important factor in encouraging pupils to develop and discuss their ideas of the 'scientific' principles involved, at an age when discussion before the whole class can prove embarrassing.

Conclusions

The use of CAL can be seen to affect the teaching-learning situation in a variety of ways. It affects not only the way in which the lessons are organised, but also the detailed structure of the events within the lesson. Many of the changes induced (or allowed) by the use of CAL have long been thought to be educationally beneficial. The most notable are the increases in small-group work and in pupil-centred discussion.

The 'coaching' episodes, which form the basis of much of the teacher–pupil interaction in the small group, provide an opportunity for the teacher to individualise the learning experience. By the appropriate use of questions, assertions, observations, etc., the teacher can respond to the needs of the individual pupil at a personal level: such responses are rarely possible in class teaching. Direct interaction allows the teacher to gain insights into the problems faced by the pupil, and allows the pupil to check and/or develop his own understanding of the topic.

The pupil–pupil dialogue which occurs when a small group of pupils are using a CAL unit is not limited to the time spent at the keyboard but can also occur during the 'data preparation' stage and during the analysis of the results. This type of dialogue is seen as particularly beneficial when the pupils are encouraged to generate and test their own hypotheses and when they are encouraged to 'explain' their ideas to each other. 'Pupil talk' forms only a *very* small part of a 'normal' lesson, and an increase in this area may prove an educationally important change in lesson structure.

An examination of the data gathered by classroom observation should immediately dispel the old myth about the computer in the classroom rendering the teacher redundant: the microcomputer is an aid to, not a replacement for, the teacher; it is the teacher who *organises* the activities of the class. At first sight this statement may seem to conflict with the claim made earlier, that the computer took on the role of task-setter. It is therefore important to distinguish between 'activities' and 'tasks'. In preparing a lesson a teacher will organise a set of activities for the class to work through: in this sense an activity may be performing a practical, taking notes or using a microcomputer. Within each activity the pupils may have to perform a number of tasks related to the activity as a whole. For example, in a 'practical' the tasks for the pupils may be to choose and assemble apparatus, control the experimental conditions, etc. It is the ability of the microcomputer to organise and control the 'tasks' that gives rise to many of the observed changes in lesson structure.

The microcomputer should not be seen as a means of minimising teacher–pupil contact – quite the reverse. By assuming the task-setting role, the micro enables the teacher to spend more time working with individual (or small groups of) pupils: exposition by the teacher (to the class) is much reduced and there is a consequent increase in the amount of pupil–teacher and pupil–pupil dialogue. This increase in small-group work can be seen to change the balance of the different types of interaction in the lesson, with a marked increase in 'coaching' episodes. These 'coaching' episodes are seen as one of the most fruitful ways in which the teacher can both assess the pupil's progress and take appropriate action. The teacher is encouraged to work in a much more supportive role: he/she is no longer simply giving instruction (in the didactic sense) but, rather, probing the pupil's understanding of the topic, reinforcing some aspects and/or extending the pupil's awareness into new areas. This more intimate teacher–pupil contact should allow the teacher to make a more accurate assessment of the difficulties faced by the individual pupil and may allow remedial action to be taken at an earlier stage than would otherwise be possible. Equally, it may allow earlier recognition of those pupils who are making rapid progress in a particular topic and so allow the teacher to provide guidance into extension work – with or without the microcomputer.

Evaluating CAL for the classroom   93

The nature of the questions used by the teacher also appears to undergo a significant change when the micro is in use. There appears to be a much greater willingness on the part of the teacher to use questions which are more open-ended and which also place a greater intellectual demand on the pupil. The reason may not lie in the structure of the programs themselves but could be a reflection of the changes in classroom organisation or teaching style which become apparent when the micro' is used. The increased demand of the questions does not appear to produce a corresponding increase in the number of incorrect responses from the pupils: it does, however, seem to generate longer responses. The pupils appear to be more willing to verbalise their thought processes – especially in the small group – and this can provide the teacher with important cues to the way in which they visualise the particular process under study. This, again, allows the teacher to take remedial action where necessary and may prove to be important in preventing erroneous concepts from being reinforced by their apparent success in dealing with particular situations.

The increase in task-related, pupil-pupil dialogue encouraged by the use of CAL may also have important consequences for the teaching-learning situation. The use of the microcomputer seems to encourage pupil work in three ways: the pupils are encouraged to discuss the reasons for their responses to the program; they are encouraged to formulate hyphotheses which enable them to predict the response of the program model; and they are encouraged to explain (to each other) their concept of the principles underlying the unit. This is not to suggest that these changes occur simply as a result of using a particular CAL unit. They must be seen as a complex function of the teaching style, the relationship between the teacher and the class, the program style and the wealth of interactions which take place in any teaching situation. However, the use of CAL provides more opportunity for these events to occur and they tend to occur more frequently than would appear to be the case in 'normal' teaching situations.

Such pupil–pupil discussions have long been believed to be important in the learning process – indeed, much class-based teacher exposition has the overt aim of generating discussion among the pupils. However, research has shown that this is rarely successful in a class situation and that the great majority of the time devoted to such discussion is, in fact, 'teacher talk': the teacher provides the descriptions, asks the questions, and often goes on to provide the answers, with little intervention from the pupils. If further observation of the use of CAL in the classroom confirms the increase in pupil–pupil dialogue, then, on those grounds alone, CAL would be making a positive contribution to the improvement of the learning environment.

In summary, observations of the use of CAL suggest that it helps to bring about a qualitatively improved learning environment in that it promotes or allows: (1) more individual or small-group work, (2) greater freedom for the teacher to discuss a topic with the pupils (as opposed to telling them about it), (3) more depth of demand in questions, (4) more open-ended questions, (5) more task-oriented pupil–pupil discussion, (6) more vocalisation, by the pupils, of their understanding of the topic being taught, (7) greater opportunity for the pupils to develop and test their own hypotheses. Further evaluation, however, is needed to establish the significance of these changes, their relative importance and their impact on the learning process.

Reference

Beeby, T., Burkhardt, H., and Fraser, R. (1979), *A Systematic Classroom Analysis Notation*. University of Nottingham: Shell Centre for Mathematical Education.

8. Computer simulations, adventure games and language development

A study of their use in the primary school

STEPHEN MOSS

This chapter is concerned with the use of microcomputers as aids to language development in the primary school, specifically to assess a childs' oral language performance and to foster oral language skills. The work was carried out over a period of three months at a four-to-nine-year First School in Walsall, and stemmed from the school's involvement in the Schools Council project 'Communication Skills 7–13'. The policy of the LEA is to involve all schools in the project on an area-by-area basis, with all staff participating in classroom observation and recording. Microcomputers would seem to have a role to play in this area, and this chapter examines the extent to which currently available materials can be used to stimulate oral communication, with the emphasis on simulation programs and adventure games.

To understand why simulations and adventure games may aid language development it is necessary to examine some current theories concerning the relationships between thought and language. Piaget (1969) has stated that the basis of all a child's learning and understanding is first-hand or concrete experience. Such experience, however, forms only part of a child's total experience, much of which can be described as social experience. Talk plays a large part in social experience.

Vygotsky (1962) shows how language and concrete experience influence one another. He points out that many concepts cannot be derived or developed from first-hand, concrete experience alone and states that language is the most potent means of helping the child to understand abstract relationships that would otherwise not be easily recognisable.

Although, stated so simply, there would appear to be conflict between Piaget and Vygotsky, both recognise the fundamental importance of language. Vygotsky sees it playing a vital part in concept *development*, whereas for Piaget its importance lies in the role it plays in increasing the range and rapidity of the power of thought.

Tough (1979) states:

> In interaction with other people talk stimulates and sets value on the child's actions; the child's actions provide the essential basis for the meanings to be attached to language; being involved in talk about his experiences leads the child to search for meaning in the talk he hears. So the child's understanding grows, supported and provoked in turn by talk, concrete experiences and action.

A Language for Life (DES, 1975) lists the following skills or uses of language which it recommends children should experience during the early years of their education:

  (i) Reporting on present and recalled experiences.
 (ii) Collaborating towards agreed ends.
(iii) Projecting into the future; anticipating and predicting.
 (iv) Projecting and comparing possible alternatives.
  (v) Perceiving causal and dependent relationships.
 (vi) Giving explanations of how and why things happen.
(vii) Expressing and recognising tentativeness.
(viii) Dealing with problems in the imagination and seeing possible solutions.
 (ix) Creating experiences through the use of imagination.
  (x) Justifying behaviour.
 (xi) Reflecting on feelings – their own and other people's.

Simulations and adventure games, by their very nature, put children in situations which require them to use many of these skills to complete a task successfully.

Simulations

Computer simulations can be any of three types: (1) programs which simulate a model or process, (2) programs which require the child to take on a role which is unfamiliar, (3) programs which contain substantial 'game' elements. Any one simulation may contain elements of all three types, but the characteristic which should distinguish an educational simulation program from other software is its ability to enable the child to participate in 'real' activities which would otherwise be too expensive, too dangerous or too time-consuming for the school to provide. There seems little point in using an expensive and powerful computer to simulate activities which can be done equally well without it, or in which the teacher could consider the practical manipulation of materials to be a significant objective.

An example of the 'process' simulation is *Lock*, which simulates the operation of a canal lock. The children are set the task of getting their boat from the top of the lock down or vice versa. To do this they need to learn the correct sequence of operations for any given state of the lock. *Mangonel* is another 'model/process' simulation which allows children to explore the effect of altering variables on the trajectory of stones fired by a medieval siege machine.

Role-playing simulations are by far the most common and can require the child to take the role of mountaineer (*Everest*), pioneer (*Westward 1847* and *Westward Ho!*), archaeologist (*Expedition to Saggara*), forest ranger, diver (*Mary Rose*) or even fox (*Suburban Fox*). These simulations can take a long time to complete and may require a change in classroom organisation to be successful. Many children find this type of simulation very interesting and become completely immersed in the role they have been asked to assume.

The third type of simulation with a strong 'gaming' element includes computer-moderated war games, and a number of 'multi-player' programs with a competitive element. I would include in this category any simulation which requires a 'winner' to emerge at the end.

There are three questions which embody the essence of a simulation:

1 *What do I do?* This is of necessity the first question the child must ask and answer. Usually you take on a role in an activity or setting which represents some particular aspect of reality. Your role in that activity will require you to make decisions and to evaluate the effect of your decisions and actions, by asking
2 *What happened?* at the end of each stage or following each decision point in the simulation. This process of evaluation is the most important aspect of using simulations in an educational setting and relates very closely to skill (i) above. It also leads on to the final question:

3 *Why did that happen?* which cannot be answered without recourse to the skills outlined in (v) and (vi) above.

Adventure games

The major characteristic which distinguishes an adventure game from a role-playing simulation is that the adventure need have no link with reality and can be purely the product of the programmer's imagination. There are two main types of adventure game; text games and graphical maze games. Maze games tend to be of rather poor quality, and so taken for present purposes any reference to adventure games can be taken to mean text-based adventures, although space ships, desert islands and subterranean caves are by far the most popular. Despite the diversity of content most text-based adventures follow the same format. The player arrives in a certain location to start the adventure. The reason for his being there may be shipwreck, escape from prison, a long search for hidden treasure or a summons from his superior to undertake a dangerous mission. One very successful and popular adventure game written specifically for children, *Granny's garden,* sets the children down in the Kingdom of the Mountains and gives them the task of finding the king and queen's six children, who have been spirited away by the wicked witch. Another popular adventure with junior-age children is *The Hobbit,* devised around the characters and events of J. R. R. Tolkien's classic.

A few adventures not written specifically for children are suitable for use in school but a program designed to keep an intelligent adult in a state of perpetual torment for several weeks would probably fail to attract or hold the attention of most children under the age of eleven.

The following transcript of the conversation between two eight year old boys and their teacher using the *Locks* simulation is a good illustration of the simulation process in action. The boys, James and Matthew are attempting to go down through the lock and have got their boat into the lock.

James. Now we want the water level to go down. (iii)
Teacher. Well, how would you get the water level to do down?
James. By opening the bottom paddle . . . (v)
Matthew. . . . . and shutting that one. (v)
Teacher. Yes, you've spotted that. You left the top one open. So which do you want to do first?
Both. Shut the top one first. (ii)

Teacher. Why?

Matthew. Because if you opened that one it would go all the way through. (v)

Teacher. Now . . . what next?

James. Open the bottom paddle.

Teacher. OK.

Matthew. James, you silly thing, we've just closed the top paddle and now you've opened it again. Let me do it.

Matthew. You need to open . . . bottom . . . paddle.

Teacher. What's happening now?

James. The water level's going down. (i)

Teacher. Why do you think the water level's going down?

Matthew. Because it's just come out of the top, and if it goes up it'll shoot all over the . . . I think . . . I don't know, really. (vii)

Teacher. What's just come out of the top? (*Pause.*) What's happened to the water that was in the lock? Where's it gone?

Matthew. It's gone into the bottom part . . . the canal bit. (i)

Teacher. That's right. Is there any water coming out of the top part now?

James. No . . . it can't, because we shut the paddle. (v)

Teacher. What do we do now?

Matthew. Open the gate, don't we? What do you think, James? (iv, ii)

James. Mm . . . yes. Open . . . bottom . . . gate.

James. It's opening . . . Look, Matt. (i)

Both. Now we want to move . . . That's 'M'. (ii)

Matthew. Now get ready to stop it. (ii)

James. Brrr . . . I'll tell you when to stop it. (ii)

Matthew. We'll probably go out of the screen. (*Giggles.*) Don't want to go too far. (ii)

James. Just go into the middle. (ii)

Matthew. That's it . . . Just there . . . by the back seat. (ii)

James. Stop! Now close . . . bottom . . . gate. (ii)

Matthew. And then we want to close the paddle as well . . . so that the water won't go running out. (iii)

James. Why does it still say 'Give command'? We've done it.

Teacher. I think you need to sail the boat away from the lock.

Matthew. OK. That's 'M'.

(*Screen shows 'Well done. You only made one mistake.'*)

Matthew. It says we made a mistake. We didn't . . . did we? I can't remember if we did or not. (vii)

James. Um . . . yes . . . I remember! We opened the top paddle after we'd already closed it (i)

The numbers in parentheses relate to the eleven categories of language use listed above.

Even within the short example above, language is used for six different purposes. As one would expect, there is no use of language for imagining or projecting. The *Lock* simulation is useful for developing language strategies i–vi but not well suited to imaginative language use.

Adventure games, however, tend to be more useful for developing those language strategies set out in vii–x above. The example below illustrates this well. A group of seven children aged eight and nine years are playing the adventure *Granny's garden*. The scenario is a search for the six children of the king and queen of the mountains. The children have been kidnapped by the wicked witch and hidden in various places. The player's task it to rescue the victims. In order to do so they must solve puzzles of increasing difficulty.

At this point the players have arrived outside the woodcutter's cottage where Esther is being held captive. Outside the cottage is an apple tree.

Simon. Well, I think we should take an apple.

Sally. No. No. Don't take one.

Teacher. Simon, why do you want to take an apple?

Rebecca. Say 'No', Simon – please.

Simon. Because . . . Well, if I go into the cottage and the witch is there . . . well, she might attack me, and I could throw the apples at her and get away.

Paul. Yes . . . That's right. I agree with Simon.

Sally. But the apples might be poisonous, and . . .

Rebecca. Yes, like in Snow White, where she eats it, like, and then she dies . . . only she's not dead, really.

Nicola. You wouldn't have to eat it, though. It might have poison on the outside, and as soon as you touch it you're dead.

David. Simon and me think we ought to take it, like, as a weapon.

Teacher. OK. You seem to be split over what to do. How shall we make a decision?

Jackie. We can have a vote . . .

David. Yeah . . . and the winner's get to choose. (*The vote is four to three in favour of taking an apple.*)

Simon. I'm going to take the apple . . . See! Nothing has happened. It's not poison.

Rebecca. It might be slow poison.

(*The players enter the cottage and find a stick by the wall.*)

Teacher. Do you want to take the stick? What do you think, Jackie?

Jackie. Well, it might be a trap. The witch will have made lots of traps,

Computers and language development   101

won't she? . . . It might be like . . . If you touch the wood a trap-door opens and you fall in.

Sally. Leave the stick. It's a trap.

David. But we'll need a stick to fight the witch. I know, if you stand away from the stick and just touch it . . . then if there's a door you won't get caught in it.

Sally. But it could be like a handle for the trap-door.

Nicola. Let's have another vote. I say take the stick.

(The vote is five to two in favour of taking the stick.)

Nicola. Right. I'll type 'Yes' and get the stick . . . *We've* got it! It's all right, see. (i)

(The players are faced with a choice of actions. They can look upstairs, or in a cupboard, the front room, they back room or the kitchen. They cannot agree.)

Teacher. I think we should let one person decide what we do next. Then if they get it wrong we can blame them, can't we? Who wants to be first?

Simon. I say to look in the kitchen.

Teacher. All right. Let's see. Just type 'Kitchen'.

Simon. It says that there's a big huge pot over the fire. Do you want to look in it? It might be another trap. (iii)

Paul. Esther could be in the pot and . . . (iii)

David. I know. The witch has tied her hands up and put plasters over her mouth so she can't shout for help. (ix).

Teacher. Do you think Esther is in the pot, Jackie?

Jackie. It says 'a huge pot', doesn't it? She might be cooking inside it. The water might be bubbling. (iv).

Sally. Ugh!

Teacher. Do you want to look in the pot?

Nicola. Well, we might fall in . . . (iii)

David. You could use the stick . . . like . . . lift the pot off the fire with the stick and put in on the floor, and then you can see in it without leaning over. (viii)

Rebecca. Yes. That's a good idea. We can do that. (ii)

Teacher. No, you can't.

David. Why not? Why can't we?

Teacher. The question is just 'Do you want to look in the pot?' You must answer 'Yes' or 'No'.

David. But it might be dangerous. (iii)

Teacher. You must weigh the dangers against the chance of rescuing Esther. Do you think Esther is in the pot?

Sally. Yes, and she might be dying. (iii)

Paul. We promised the king and queen we'd help them. (x)

David. We didn't promise. It just said, 'Do you want to help them?. (x)

Teacher. I think we ought to vote. Don't you?

(The vote is four to three in favour of looking in the pot.)

Sally. I'll type it . . . Oh, *no!*
(*The witch appears and captures the players.*)
David. I told you! I told you! Now we've got to start again. (v)

This transcript can give only a glimpse of the excitement, concentration and total involvement which the children displayed in playing the game. They slipped into role very quickly and followed up this failure with a successful attempt to rescue Esther, who had been changed into a broom and hidden in a cupboard.

The situations created by this particular game drew imaginative thought from the children and encouraged them to express their thoughts clearly.

Classroom organisation

In order for simulations and adventure games to be used successfully as a means of fostering language development the classroom must be organised appropriately. In the course of this study it became apparent that the optimum group size was six or seven children. With fewer than this there was a danger of one dominant personality emerging and submerging the others. Larger groups meant that some children made a very small contribution. Teachers found it easy to involve all the children in a group of six or seven and to sustain talk for longer periods.

The group of seven children who played *Granny's garden* in the transcript above spent over fifty minutes in continuous conversation and had completed only a quarter of the adventure. The teacher, in this case, sat with the group whilst a colleague worked with the rest of the class. Such an arrangement would not be possible in most primary classrooms, and so the group would have to play unsupervised. Some teachers find this difficult to accept. Comments such as 'How do I know they're doing it right?' and 'What have they got to show for it?' are frequently heard. It requires a great act of faith on the part of many teachers to leave a group of children to work through a simulation or adventure for a long period of time at the end of which they may have 'failed' to complete the task successfully. The teacher cannot mark or grade their work. There may be nothing written down.

The results of this study show that teachers have little to fear. Without exception the groups worked and played hard and with total concentration over extended periods of time. Tape-recordings of sessions when the teacher was not present showed no falling-off in involvement or concentration, although groups sometimes got bogged down in arguments over decisions to be taken. Groups where a teacher had introduced the voting method of decision-making tended to continue the practice when left to their own devices.

As for record-keeping, a tape recorder can be left running during the session and the contents analysed by the teacher another time. Transcripts can be made if the teacher so desires.

It was found that groups using simulations and adventure games produced considerable amounts of associated work – written and pictorial – and time had to be set aside for the children to produce these more considered responses to the programs.

References

Department of Education and Science (1975), *A Language for Life* (the Bullock Report). London: HMSO.

Piaget, J., and Inhelder, B. (1969), *The Psychology of the Child*. London: Routledge.

Tough, J. (1979), *Talk for Teaching and Learning*. London: Ward Lock.

Vygotsky, L. S. (1962), *Thought and Language*. New York: Wiley.

Software

Simulations

Everest, TRS-80 Educational Users Group. *Expedition to Saggara*, Ginn. *Forest ranger*, TRS-80 Educational Users' Group. *Lock*, Andrew Tapsfield, MAPE. *Mangonel*, David Harris, MAPE. *Mary Rose*, Ginn. *Suburban fox*, Ginn. *Westward ho!* and *Westward 1847*, both TRS-80 Educational Users' Group.

Adventure games

Adventureland, Adventure International. *Granny's garden*, 4mat Software. *The hobbit*, Melbourne House. *Pirate adventure*, Adventure International.

9. Microcompters in physics

DIGBY G. SWIFT

If anyone ought to be at home with the school microcomputer it is the physics teacher. More specifically, it is that (unfortunately by no means ubiquitous) member of the physics staff with competence and enthusiasm in the field of microelectronics. He is the one who understands what is going on inside the computer, and how to connect it to other electronic equipment. His flair for electronics is usually coupled with a flair for programming. He may well have been on the scene at the beginning with his self-assembled KIM-1 or other early hobbeyist computer. He also had the benefit of much of the early (e.g. 'Chelsea') software, and the first definitive text on the use of microcomputers in a school subject, namely R. A. Sparkes, *Microcomputers in Science Teaching* (1982).

How then are these 'microelectronics enthusiasts' using their microcomputers? Do they use them in the majority of their lessons (as some seem to feel all teachers will one day)? Do they use them for individual and group work as well as with the class as a whole? Are they well supplied with equipment and the latest software? In an attempt to answer these questions, and, more generally, to investigate the overall activity of these teachers in the field of micro-electronics and computing, the author carried out a small survey in early 1983 and (mainly as follow-up visits) in mid-1984, visiting schools in South and West Yorkshire whose physics departments had a reputation in this field. In all, twelve schools were visited, each having been recommended by teachers and lecturers attached to the Micro-electronics Education Programme. Three of these schools were grammar schools, six were comprehensives with a sixth form and three were comprehensive schools without a sixth form. In six of the schools the head of physics was interviewed. In the remainder the respondent was another member of the department who was the major source of innovation, and of the school's reputation, in the field of micro-electronics and computing. This chapter is based on the results of these interviews (so far as they relate to microcomputing), together with the observations and personal experience of the author. Whilst the small size of the survey means that we cannot generalise the results, nevertheless they should give some pointers as to the way microcomputers are, and should be, used in school physics departments, and some of the problems involved.

A wealth of possibilities

Before considering how microcomputers *are* being used in school physics departments it may be best first to consider how they *might* be used. There are many possibilities, most of which fall into one of the following categories.

First of all, there are the traditional 'programmed learning' or 'tutorial' programs. Pupils are led through a set of 'lessons', the computer testing their knowledge at each stage and directing them accordingly. Although computers had been used in this way before the arrival of the micro, examples are still comparatively rare. Sparkes, who gives one such program, entitled *Resistors in series and parallel*, suggests that the shortage is due to the amount of effort and skill needed to write a successful package. Programs of this nature are also somewhat limited in that they are intended for use by an individual pupil. This implies the need for a roomful of machines, although a single machine might, for example, enable a child who has missed some lessons to catch up with the others.

Another category of program is the individualised drill-and-practice routine. The computer has several possible advantages over the textbook. It gives immediate feedback, perhaps with some form of visual or aural reinforcement of success, and the provision of information to avoid repeated failure. It can also adjust the level of difficulty to the individual child and can increase the range of questions by means of the random-number generator. Such programs are relatively easy to write and are therefore quite common, especially in the field of mathematics. Unfortunately, as with the tutorial programs, their use implies the availability of a large number of machines.

This direct, 'closed' type of instruction and testing is not the only way the computer can impart knowledge. It can use a more open-ended investigative approach. An important example is the mathematical simulation of physical phenomena, presenting the information in an easily digested visual display. The simulation may be of an experiment in physics or a 'real-life' application of the physical principles. Programs may require the pupils to make decisions and observe their effects, or alternatively may allow investigations of the 'What would happen if I changed the value of this variable?' type. Such programs can be in the form of a game, trying to reach a high score or 'beat the computer'. They are normally intended to be used with groups of two to four pupils, but some are also suitable for use with the whole class. Several commercial physics programs adopt this approach, including some in the Longman's and Fiveways series. The program *Slick!* is a good example of a real-life simulation set in the form of a game.

In terms of class teaching the most obvious way of using a microcomputer is as an 'electronic blackboard'. The computer is particularly good at drawing diagrams, and has the advantage of animation. Unlike the film projector, it allows for interaction. The teacher can go at his or her own pace, and choose which parts of the diagram to change or animate as the lesson proceeds. There are not many commercial programs in this category, although Sparkes (1982) provides a few, including wave interference, molecular motion and the movement of electrical charges.

Another obvious use of the computer is as a calculator, either for students in a practical class or for the teacher when going through a problem on the board. Thompson (1983) speaks of the numerical insight given by using the computer to evaluate an equation for a large number of numerical values. He also notes the possibility of using more realistic assumptions – for example, air resistance in projectile motion – that would lead to unacceptable numerical calculations without the computer. The computer can also display the results of its calculation in graphical form or in any other desired form. A good example of a commercial program that could be placed in this category is the Cambrige Microsoftware program *Watts in your home*.

One of the major uses of a computer in everyday life is to run a data base. There are several possibilities for this in science, for example the data file of the elements in the *Quest-D* and *Microquery* packages. Such data bases can also be used to hold student records, inventory lists and other administrative records.

A word-processing package can be used for producing and updating experiment guides, pupil hand-outs and other documents that require minor changes from time to time.

Finally, the microcomputer can be 'interfaced' with other laboratory equipment to take measurements and control electrical equipment, either in a teacher demonstration or as a class experiment. As Thompson (1983) points out, this is one of the most fruitful areas of application for the physics teacher. It is also one of the most interesting. These, then, are the main ways that microcomputers can be used by school physics departments. How they are used will depend on many considerations. One factor will be the number and types of microcomputers available and the presence of certain associated peripherals. Let us first, therefore, examine the equipment that was available to the schools visited in 1983.

Equipment

When is a computer not a computer? Answer: when it's a microprocessor system being used to teach control. In physics departments a tally of the number and types of computers available needs to be preceded by the question 'What do you mean by a microcomputer?' According to one commonly used definition, a computer is a processing unit (e.g. a microprocessor) together with the items needed to link it to the outside world. These do not have to include a conventional keyboard or a cathode-ray display. Indeed, many industrial applications of computers, and many of the microprocessors used in school physics departments, involve neither.

If, however, we limit our attention to the conventional image of the school microcomputer that involves a typewriter-style keyboard and a monitor or television screen, then the computers available to physics staff in early 1983 and the number of schools possessing them were as follows: BBC (eleven schools); Sharp 380Z (six schools); Sinclair ZX81 (4 schools); Sharp (two schools); Pet (one school); Apple (one school); Nascom (one school); Video Genie (one school); Sinclair Spectrum (one school in 1983; more in 1984).

There are several points to notice here. Firstly, few of these machines were based within the physics department. Most schools had a permanent computer base containing at least the majority of the school machines, including the computer supplied under the DOI scheme. This base was used mainly for computer studies and information technology or computer awareness courses. Only in seven schools were there additional computers based within the physics department, and then only one or two machines. Needless to say, it was in these schools that the physics department was making greatest use of the computer, the other schools having to contend with timetabling difficulties and the problems of transferring equipment between the computer base and the physics department.

A second point to notice is the wide range of computers being used (matched, incidentally, by an equal variety of electronics kits). From the 1984 visits it was obvious that there is now a tendency to concentrate on one machine, usually the BBC microcomputer despite, in most cases, the absence of a disc drive for this machine. (This was also noted in the 1984 Educational Computing survey.) The reasons given were a personal preference for the machine and the difficulty of switching from one machine to another. In one particular school (and in others the author had heard about but been unable to visit) there was an emphasis not on the BBC but on the small Sinclair machines. This was partly a matter of cost but more especially because these were the machines the pupils were using at home. Indeed, the pupils were encouraged to bring their own computers to school (a policy shared by some of the other schools). Despite this trend, it is evident that teachers often have an investment in programs and skills in connection with their original machines. It is also unlikely that they will soon feel they have sufficient BBCs or Spectrums (Spectra?) to discard their original purchases, especially as there will be strong pressure for any new machines purchased by the school to go to the computer base. It appears likely, therefore, that some of the physics departments will be using a wide range of computers for some time to come.

Two opposing views were expressed concerning the networking of the school computers. Some were in favour, one department seeking a separate network specially for the science departments, with disc drive and printer based in the preparation room for security reasons. Other departments favoured a collection of self-contained microcomputers on trolleys, each with its own disc drive. However, in most cases such plans were in the future, few departments possessing a disc drive or a printer. Indeed, the only other peripherals seemed to be those made as student projects, the interfaces to be referred to later and, in one school, an EPROM programmer for the BBC.

Finance was, inevitably, a problem in all schools, some finding a partial solution in the acquisition of second-hand equipment, for example unwanted black-and-white television sets from parents and old teletype terminals for use as printers. Nevertheless, nobody expressed severe problems due to lack of equipment. A much greater problem was that of time!

Using the microcomputer

Foster (1982) noted, in a survey carried out in Havering, that the schools using micros in science tended to be those which offered both computer studies and electronics in the curriculum. This was also true in the author's survey, if by 'computer studies' (taken as an examination subject by only a few of the schools) we include 'computer awareness' and 'information technology'. In the author's case this phenomenon had a simple explanation: the electronics enthusiast in many of the physics departments spent much of his time and most of his enthusiasm in teaching these other courses. His use of the microcomputer in physics lessons, at least for measurement and control, tended to be a spin-off from these other activities! Six of the schools had introduced lower-school computer awareness courses in which this member of the physics staff was involved. Other schools were considering the possibility. In a few, but only a few, of the departments visited, a micro-electronics module was also being introduced into the early parts of the physics course, leading up to an appreciation of the microcomputer for 'control' applications. It seemed unfortunate that it was the pupils destined for A level that were unable to follow these courses through to age sixteen-plus. This was either because of the absence of digital electronics within the O level syllabus or, in the case of the JMB sixteen-plus course that does have an electronics option, the need to choose the more mathematical 'further physics for today's world' option as a preparation for the rigours of A level! Even in the sixth form the teacher interested in electronics had to express this interest mainly outside the physics course. In at least two cases the conflict between an interest in electronics as an important area of applied physics and the need for pupils to succeed in a physics course almost devoid of electronics seems to have been a source of tension between the 'enthusiast' and his head of department.

In all but two of the physics departments the 'electronics

enthusiast' was helping pupils in an out-of-hours computing or electronics 'club'. This often seemed to be where the real action was, where the teacher was most readily able to share his enthusiasm with the pupils. However, it also seemed to be placing a severe demand on the teacher's time. Many teachers were arriving at school an hour early, leaving two hours after lessons had finished, and working through their lunch hour. Despite this tendency for the 'action' to take place outside the main physics courses, these staff are nevertheless active in using microcomputers within their physics teaching, though not to the extent one might expect.

Microcomputers in some areas of school life have been described by sceptics – or are they realists? – as 'an expensive luxury' and 'a solution looking for a problem'. This could not be said of the computers used by the physics departments visited by the author. The computers were used only when there was a real need, and their cost was not excessive in comparison with the alternatives.

The major needs satisfied by the computer were: (1) the provision of controllable animated diagrams to illustrate difficult physical concepts, (2) a device to assist the teacher with demonstrations involving difficult measurements, for example those involving a very short time span, and (3) to assist the teacher in processing and displaying the results of an experiment or a worked example. This meant that, in the schools visited, the computer was mainly used as (1) an 'electronic blackboard', (2) a calculator with graphical display, and (3) a 'data logger' used to measure and store the values of physical variables.

One school was using the computer for manipulating a data base, and again there was an emphasis on this being a response to a need and not a solution looking for a problem. In this case the need was to demonstrate the statistical nature of measurements, taking as examples of the latter some physical dimensions of the pupils. The class soon appreciated the need for a computer to assist in handling, and obtaining meaning from, this collection of data.

Little use was as yet being made of word-processing and administrative packages, though this was felt to constitute a real, if low-priority, need that departments would be considering in the future.

For those schools teaching digital electronics within the physics syllabus the computer was a useful end point, enabling the pupils to perform interesting control projects simulating real-life applications of electronics. In most cases the 'computer' used was a machine-code microprocessor system such as the Unilab 'one-bit' microprocessor board, the Microprofessor, or, in one case, a microprocessor board designed and made by the teacher concerned. Occasionally, however, the conventional microcomputer was used for this purpose.

The only other significant example of students using the computer in a physics class seemed to be at the few schools where A level students were using a single computer to simulate an otherwise impracticable experiment, or as part of a real experiment, in a practical class. The other categories of program – tutorial programs, drill-and-practice routines and simulations for individual or group use – were not in evidence in physics classes (though they were used, especially simulations, in information technology and computer awareness courses). Those asked about it pointed out that there was too little time within the teaching of physics to include such items. The only place where they could be of obvious benefit would be in slack periods after exams and, for example, when part of the class were away on a visit with another teacher. Enjoyable game-type simulations would then be of benefit, given access to sufficient microcomputers. This was felt to be an area of low priority compared with the need to reinforce class teaching of difficult concepts in mainstream physics lessons. Some simulations, for example of Millikan's experiment, were, however, occasionally used with the class as a whole.

Software

Perhaps the most striking, and to the author the most surprising, finding was the almost complete rejection of commerical software. 'Written by programmers for programmers,' 'Seen but not used,' 'Not suitable below A level,' and 'Rubbish!' were some of the comments. The only commercial CAL program being used by more than one school was the Fiveways program on lenses. As many of the teachers admitted, their knowledge of commercial programs available was limited. It is unfortunate that, presumably owing to concern about illicit copying, the 'inspection copy' system used for textbooks does not apply to software; in a market felt to be full of shoddy goods, teachers are unwilling to risk purchasing programs they have not seen. The local MEP office or LEA computing centre ought to have been a way round the problem, but few if any seemed to be using it.

The major problems here was stated to be the lack of time, and in some cases the travelling distances involved.

The bulk of the programs used were: (1) those written by teachers in the department, (2) programs written by teachers from other schools belonging to a local computer users' club or science teachers' group (but not, so far as could be seen, equivalent MEP 'blue file' non-copyright programs from the MEP), (3) programs copied from computer magazines, and (4) programs written by pupils, in collaboration with a member of the physics staff. The last of these has obvious benefits. It saves the teacher time, thereby overcoming the often raised criticism that teachers are there to teach and not to write programs. Furthermore it draws on the programming abilities of the pupils, which are sometimes well beyond those of the teacher, and – most important of all – it reinforces the pupils' knowledge of that particular area of science in a way that is possible only through using it as the basis of a program.

The author suspects that the main reason teachers wrote their own programs was because they enjoyed doing it. However, there are other obvious benefits. The teacher produces just what he needs to use, and is fully confident in using it. The commercial programs are sometimes longer and more sophisticated than is necessary to illustrate a particular topic in physics – to some extent, they have to be to justify their cost! Indeed, the most effective programs can sometimes be the short and simple routines written in front of the class with the assistance of the pupils. Fletcher (1983) noted with regret the virtual absence of such programs in the mathematics classes he visited. At least some of the physics departments the author visited were taking advantage of the computer in this way, and mainly for the more mathematical aspects of physics.

As regards the general use of the computer as an electronic blackboard, the topic that was illustrated more than any other was wave behaviour, and in particular the superimposition of waves. This was expected. It is a conceptually difficult topic, difficult to explain using chalk-and-talk yet also difficult to demonstrate effectively in any other way. On the other hand it is a problem for which the modern microcomputer might almost have been designed, so effectively does it display the information for so little in the way of programming. Optical ray diagrams are equally effective on the computer, but not quite so easy to program – hence, presumably, the relative success of the Fiveways lenses program. A third important example is charge flow in an electric circuit. (Basic tends to be too slow for this to be really effective. A machine code version produced by one teacher was infinitely superior. Unfortunately the work involved, even using an assembler, is phenomenal, and, once written, the program cannot easily be translated for use on another machine. Hardware and software developments, such as the *Melbourne draw* package for the Spectrum used by one teacher, should help alleviate this problem.) Other examples include projectile motion, the working of an internal combustion engine, molecular motion, alpha particle scattering, and so on.

Many departments were using the computer to draw graphs and charts, for example in connection with radioactive decay (changing sample times to illustrate the smoothing out of random scatter) and the discharge of a capacitor. These were most effective when linked directly to measurements on a real capacitor, and this brings us to the next point – the use of computers for measurement and control.

Interfacing

When the microcomputer is used for measurement or control it is usually necessary to provide an interface, if only to protect the computer from excessive voltages. A variety of commercial interfaces have been available for some time, but one striking and surprising feature of the author's 1983 survey was that every department except one had either constructed its own or had one constructed by another teacher. This do-it-yourself activity has been criticised: surely it is a waste of the teachers' time, and results in an inferior product? The teachers would argue that commercial interfaces, at the time, were expensive and not particularly well attuned to their needs. The making of an interface also provided some of them with a chance to practise newly learned skills in practical electronics. In 1984 the position seems to have changed, mainly because of the advent of two inexpensive and highly versatile commercial interfaces: the Interspec for the Spectrum and ZX81, and the Vela.

The DoI/MEP-sponsored *V*ersatile *La*boratory instrument or Vela (see Lambert, 1983) is not by any means just a computer interface. It is, in effect, itself a computer, able to take measurements of time, frequency or voltages over a wide range of values far quicker than a normal computer and with a minimum of effort. It is designed to be capable of operating as a data logger on its own, with its own display, and those schools that had it were using it in that way. However, some of them were also using it as an intelligent and versatile BBC interface, and those schools just recieving it tended to see it as the solution to many of their problems in regard to the use of computers for measuring, storing, processing and displaying scientific measurements.

All departments saw the interfacing of the computer to the 'real world' as an important future development. Two examples already in operation have been mentioned. Others included the measurement of gravity by free fall, trolley and air-track experiments, and Kirchoff's laws with changing voltages. Control systems such as robot arms, various types of 'buggy', traffic lights, a bar-code reader, etc., were sometimes demonstrated in physics classes, though their main use was in electronics and technology courses.

Conclusions

Several conclusions could be drawn. I will deal with two, one positive and the other negative. One thing that appears evident is that, even in the hands of electronics enthusiasts, we are not going to see physics classes based in a roomful of computers carrying out simulated experiments and other forms of second-hand science. Although even the front-runners interviewed were just starting to make use of the computer, they were highly critical both of software and of poor teaching methods. It seems unlikely that they will ever use the computer to measure, demonstrate or otherwise deal with items better covered in some other way. The computer is meeting real needs and should have an all-round beneficial effect on physics teaching. Only objective tests of pupils' understanding, attainment and attitudes can really confirm the effectiveness of the microcomputer in the schools. Nevertheless, after the demonstrations I have seen involving, for example, the Vela as a BBC interface for demonstrating radioactive decay, I for one have no doubts.

My other point concerns the excessive reliance that seems to be placed on so few enthusiastic, skilled and overworked individuals in the physics department, not just for introducing microcomputers and micro-electronics into the teaching of physics but also for introducing or helping with so many more IT-related courses within the school. One obvious consequence is the precarious nature of the school's involvement (and reputation) in this field. Many of the teachers interviewed wondered what would happen to the work they had built up if they were to leave. (I was told that the MEP absorbed several such people, and TVEI and recruitment to the LEA advisory service are no doubt having the same effect.) It is difficult enough to find good physics teachers of any variety today, and especially electronics experts who are willing to devote so much of their own time to the school. Whatever the solution – providing more and better equipment and in-service courses to enable other members of staff to contribute, or introducing more favourable conditions of service – something needs to be done. A computer in every school was a good first step. Obtaining suitable software is another. The major need however, is the encouragement of more able and enthusiastic teachers to enter the profession and support these important new developments.

References

Fletcher, T. J. (1983), *Microcomputers and Mathematics in Schools*, London: Department of Education and Science.

Foster, S. (1982), 'One year's progress in Havering', *Educational Computing*, September.

Lambert, A. (1983), 'The development of Vela: an asset in any science lab', *Educational Computing*, July/August.

Sparkes, R. A. (1982), *Microcomputers in Science Teaching*, London: Hutchinson.

Thompson, D. (1983), 'Has the micro a real place in school physics?, *Educational Computing*, December/January.

10. Microcomputers and mathematics

NEIL STRAKER

The microcomputer in the mathematics lesson

The arrival of microcomputers in secondary schools would at first sight appear to be of great benefit to those who teach mathematics. The microcomputer can act as a valuable teaching and learning aid. If the graphics of the machine are fully exploited, extremely effective demonstrations can be performed, for example in transformation geometry or graphical interpretation. The microcomputer can also be used to handle large amounts of data in statistical work, particularly at A level.

> There can be no doubt that the increasing availability of microcomputers in schools offers considerable opportunity to teachers of mathematics both to enhance their existing practice and also to work in ways which have not hitherto been possible. In particular, the availability of a visual display offers many possibilities for the imaginative pictorial presentation of mathematical work of many kinds. [Cockcroft (1982), para. 402]

> At the secondary stage we believe that there is a special need to develop the potentiality of the high-resolution graphical display which is now available on many microcomputers. This enables work to be done on graph-plotting and, at a higher level, can be used to provide a visual presentation of basic ideas in calculus and of the use of iterative methods to solve equations. Many geometrical properties can also be demonstrated in ways which have hitherto only been possible using cine-films. [*Ibid.*, para. 411]

There is perhaps even greater value in the short five or ten-line program which the teacher can type in, with the help of the pupils, during the course of a lesson. This type of approach requires little in the way of programming expertise and is a possibility which all mathematics departments ought to explore. Fletcher (1983) also emphasises this type of computer use in his *Microcomputers and Mathematics in Schools:* 'You know that you have really grasped a mathematical process if you can program a machine to perform it. This implies a style of teaching which, at the moment, is hardly to be found' (para. 62). For example, if pupils are able to assist in the production of a short computer program which will test whether a given whole number is prime, they must have a complete understanding of what is meant by a prime number. In addition, the mathematical discussion which would accompany this exercise would be of great value.

The writer has recently seen a number of student teachers using short programs of this nature in a way which provides an added dimension to the teaching of mathematics.

1. One teacher introduced probability by discussing the spinning of a coin. The children were then required to carry out a simple coin spinning experiment. In order to produce a larger number of trials a program was typed into the computer, which simulated the experiment. The computer results were then used as a basis for discussion on simple ideas of limits, expected number of heads and whether the coin has a 'memory'. The same program was also used with a group of sixth-form statistics students who were being introduced to the idea of confidence limits.

2. One interesting lesson was observed where sixth-form students were asked to consider the area under the curve $y=1/x$. A program was used which calculated various areas via the trapezium rule, and it was observed that the resulting area function behaved as a logarithmic function. This led on to an area investigation which resulted in the discovery of the constant e and the exponential function. In this particular case the computer program was very simple but made the numerical aspect much less tedious.

3. In another lesson a student used a graph-plotting program which he himself had written to demonstrate quickly the salient features of the quadratic function to a group of fourth-year pupils. He was thus able to demonstrate how the sign of the discriminant affected the graph of the function. Such a program is also of immense value at sixth form level when studying topics such as differentiation, maxima and minima, conic sections, and in teaching curve sketching.

4. The microcomputer was used with one group of sixth-formers to simulate the decomposition of a chemical compound, as an

introduction to first-order differential equations.

5. The microcomputer was also used in investigation work, where pupils had been introduced to certain investigations using pencil-and-paper methods and were then using a computer program to speed up the calculation process.

In all these examples the programs were written by the student teachers, often with the help of the class. It would not be reasonable, however, to expect all mathematics teachers to write more complex programs. Such work is extremely time-consuming, especially if the programs are to be used by other teachers. A possible solution is for groups of teachers within an area to form writing groups so that software can be shared among a number of schools.

> Programs come from a variety of sources. A lot of material is available in some LEA resource centres, and many lessons use material which schools have obtained through this channel. In many cases teachers have written their own programs. It is common to hear the advice that program writing is a matter for experts and that teachers should leave the matter to others; but many mathematics teachers have demonstrated their ability to write serviceable programs which meet their needs at least as well as programs written elsewhere. These programs would often need foolproofing and better documentation if they were to be transferred to other users, but for the moment they serve their purposes excellently. [Fletcher (1983), para. 40]

Commercial programs have been criticised on many counts, but there is now some software available for mathematics, admittedly rather expensive, which can be of value in the classroom.

Unfortunately the microcomputer is rarely used in the mathematics classroom. Few mathematics departments have their own machine, and are unable to gain access to a microcomputer because of the demands on machine time by computer studies departments. Computer studies also make another, more serious demand, namely that of requiring large numbers of mathematics teachers to teach computer studies to CSE, O and A levels.

> Even in schools in which computer studies courses are well established and are taught by those who teach mathematics, the use which is made in the mathematics classroom of the computer facilities which are available seems often to be very limited. [Cockcroft (1982), para 405]

Furthermore it appears that in some schools mathematics teaching time is given up in order to allow computer awareness courses to appear on the timetable. While not questioning the need for awareness courses or examination courses in computer studies, the need to divert specialist teachers of mathematics towards this area must be a cause of concern.

The growth of computer studies

Computer studies first appeared on the secondary school curriculum in the 1960s. The arrival of the microcomputer in both the home and the school together with the publicity which accompanied the Department of Industry schemes has led to a rapid growth of interest in the subject. From the teacher's point of view the need for batch processing of programs has all but disappeared. Computer studies has instant appeal for many pupils, who see it as an up-to-date course which will involve a considerable amount of machine use. In reality the subject is perhaps a little less attractive, with O level syllabuses also containing sections on the evolution of computer systems, descriptive treatment of hardware, logic, implications of computerisation for society and applications of computing. There has been some criticism of the content of O level computer studies courses.

> Because they were developed in circumstances different from those now prevailing most present courses now require revision. They do not encourage practical application of the new technology. Courses often deal in a superficial way with social implications which require a greater sophistication than is exhibited by the majority of 16 year olds. The emphasis is mainly on theoretical applications of computers with particular emphasis on automatic data processing, so that it is possible for students to pass without programming or even coming into contact with a real machine. Current practice takes little advantage of the exciting world of microelectronics in which we are now living and it will be a serious loss if the new sixteen-plus examinations remove those elements which made the original syllabuses so stimulating to both teachers and pupils. [Fletcher (1983), para. 76]

Thorne (1983) also suggests that computer studies is failing to come up to expectations:

> But if the government's aim was to strengthen our imagination and thinking on information technology at school level, existing computer studies courses at CSE, O and A level are doing little to fulfil that expectation. With a very few welcome exceptions our current computer

studies examination syllabuses are still, despite a recent and continuing Secondary Examinations Council review, out of date, intellectually undemanding and lacking in that most crucial of all computing concepts, critical awareness.

Nevertheless the subject does recruit particularly well at all levels in secondary schools, and continues to grow in popularity, as Table 1 shows.

Table 1 Examination entries: number of candidates taking computer studies, 1975–83

Year	CSE	O	AO	A	CEE	Total
1975	8,785	1,335	–	1,340	–	11,460
1976	13,181	3,217	116	1,512	–	18,026
1977	15,218	6,091	109	1,764	–	23,182
1978	15,489	8,417	511	1,769	233	26,419
1979	16,210	11,635	765	2,323	591	31,524
1980	17,901	14,907	1,049	2,819	635	37,311
1981	23,590	22,546	1,374	3,947	1,250	52,707
1982	32,261	37,868	1,524	5,825	1,531	79,007
1983	44,653	50,219	2,143	7,310	3,180	107,505

Source: ICL/CES *Newsletter*.

The increasing acceptance of computer studies as a subject for more academic pupils is evident from the table when it is noted that since 1982 O level entries have exceeded CSE entries. The total entry for 1985 shows a threefold increase on the 1980 figure which coincides with the introduction of microcomputers into all secondary schools through the DoI scheme and with the arrival of the BBC Model B machine on the market. Wellington (1983) demonstrates that computer studies is now an established school subject when he notes that the number of computer studies examination entries nationally far exceeds the total German entry, and will soon reach the level of French. It is certain that this total entry will continue to grow in future years, especially if we take account of the substantial computing element in vocational education courses such as TVEI.

The staffing of computer studies

Graduates in computer science are not being attracted towards careers in schoolteaching. It would appear that more rewarding and challenging careers lie elsewhere, in industry and commerce. In

1983–84 only thirty-one students following computing as a main course at PGCE level. The secondary BEd in computing is perhaps an alternative route into computing teaching, but there appears to be little prospect of healthy recruitment into such courses, few of which are in existence.

The Cockcroft Report (DES, 1982) alerted us to the link which has evolved between mathematics and computer studies in terms of staffing:

> It [computer studies] was developed largely by teachers of mathematics and in many schools there would at the present time be no computer studies in the curriculum at all if mathematicians did not undertake the teaching. For this reason, many people both within the education system and outside it have assumed that computer studies should be regarded as the responsibility of mathematics departments. [para. 396]

Fletcher (1983) also notes the existence of the staffing link:

> The Cockcroft Report drew attention to the likelihood that a significant proportion of the teaching of computer studies will be undertaken by mathematics teachers who will in consequence have less time available to teach mathematics. More recent experience serves only to underline this warning. Some new entrants to teaching have specialised in computer science rather than mathematics, but they are still a small proportion of the whole. In the majority of cases computer studies are being taught by teachers who might otherwise be teaching mathematics and/or science. [para. 119]

Such a link is perhaps seen as natural, since mathematics graduates are likely to have studied computer programming as part of their degree course. While mathematicians may possess the requisite programming skills for computer studies work at school level, one danger of using mathematicians to staff school courses is that there will be too great an emphasis on mathematical programming and numerical operations. It is questionable whether a mathematician is as well suited as an arts graduate to teach the historical details, social implications and applications of the new technology.

The alliance of mathematics and computing can also be observed in job advertisements, which often refer to the ability to offer computer studies as being an added qualification. Approximately 30 per cent of all Scale 1 mathematics vacancies make reference to the teaching of computing. In the whole of 1982 more than half the Scale 1 and 2 advertisements for computing vacancies which appeared in the *Times*

Educational Supplement required mathematics to be offered as a second subject. At a more senior level many heads of mathematics are required to assume overall responsibility for computing departments.

Butterworth (1983) also notes the diversion of mathematicians into computing in his study of twenty-two schools in ten LEAs:

> Advisers said that many schools saw the work as properly within the province of the mathematics department, and that in others, scientists or mathematicians and scientists together were responsible. Advisers saw the use of mathematicians and scientists for computer studies as a threat to the availability of scarce teaching time. They spoke of encouraging schools, but with only moderate success, to seek for ways of involving a wider range of teachers. [p. 149]

Writing in the *TES*, R. W. Strong (1984), County Inspector for Mathematics, Somerset, stresses the need to release mathematicians from computing responsibilities. He cites numerous areas of computer education where mathematicians are involved: writing software, using the microcomputer in mathematics lessons, teaching computer studies, giving school-based support to staff, developing computer awareness courses, running clubs and using the microcomputer for school administration:

> With the exceptions of writing software for the enhancement of mathematical education and learning about the machine, the time being spent on these activities is now beginning to reflect adversely on the quality of work that is taking place in mathematics classrooms. Mathematics teachers are being taken out of mathematics teaching (and at times replaced by teachers of other disciplines to cover the mathematics timetable). They are also spending considerable amounts of time helping other staff at the expense of their own teaching preparation, or dealing with time-consuming technical problems. The overall effect of such activities is a deterioration in the quality of mathematics in the classroom. There is a pressing need to remove from mathematics teachers responsibility for the wider issues in computer education and microtechnology development in schools.

The problem is even more serious when one considers that mathematics is a shortage subject which can ill afford to lose staffing expertise to another area. Mathematics teaching needs staff who have ideas and show initiative, and yet it is invariably teachers with these qualities who have seized the opportunity to move into a field which will broaden their experience and therefore increase their promotion prospects. The Cockcroft Report estimated that the full-time equivalent of approximately 600 teachers of mathematics were diverted into computer studies teaching. A more recent survey (Straker, 1983) was based on questionnaire replies from 103 heads of mathematics in secondary schools in north-east and north-west England. In 83 per cent of the schools in the sample, mathematics teachers were involved in the teaching of computer studies, while 55 per cent of heads of mathematics had overall responsibility for computing. A mean full-time equivalent of 0·42 mathematics teacher per school was teaching computing, which, projected nationally for secondary schools in England and Wales, would represent a total of approximately 1,900 mathematics teachers. While it is recognised that this is only a crude projection, the growth in examination entries over the last three years would suggest a reasonable degree of accuracy in the estimated figure. The figure of 1,900 mathematicians is over three times the Cockcroft estimate, and is supported by the threefold increase in examination entries which occurred in the interval between the two estimates.

A more detailed survey (Straker, 1983) of computer studies provision in one LEA was undertaken in December 1983, with submissions received from twelve of the fourteen secondary schools in the authority. This work was followed up by discussions and interviews with a number of heads of mathematics in the LEA. The results showed that 86 per cent of the computer studies teaching in the twelve schools was in the hands of mathematics specialists, the computing courses requiring a staffing equivalent of 0·89 mathematics teacher per school. Eight of the nine designated heads of computing in the survey schools were mathematics specialists, and four of the nine heads of computing were also second in mathematics departments. Only 14 per cent of the computing taught was in the form of awareness courses, the majority of the teaching being to CSE, O and A level. In general the heads of mathematics felt that computing courses should not be associated with mathematics departments only.

It was also found in four of the twelve schools that mathematics teaching time was taken up so that computer awareness courses could operate. In most schools microcomputers were not available for mathematics lessons, so that the use of the microcomputer as a teaching aid was virtually non-existent. At the time of the survey there were two mathematics vacancies in the authority which were unlikely to be filled, yet there was undoubted a surplus of mathematics specialists within the LEA; it was deployed to teach computer studies.

The views of the heads of mathematics

In general the comments made by the heads of mathematics in discussions suggested that they would willingly dispense with the computing responsibility. The following specific points can be made as a result of the interviews:

1. In some schools the deployment of mathematicians to teach computer studies meant that mathematics classes, usually in the first or second year, were taught by non-mathematicians, many of whom were reluctant to teach the subject. Five heads of department specifically stated that the diversion of mathematics specialists into computing was having a detrimental effect on the quality of teaching within the mathematics department: these were cases where non-specialists were required to teach mathematics.

2. Heads of department were experiencing difficulty in involving their second-in-department in the running of the mathematics department in those schools where the second-in-mathematics also had responsibility for computing.

3. Heads of department felt that the trend of mathematicians taking on more and more computer studies teaching would continue in the foreseeable future. The introduction of TVEI courses, which require a substantial computing input, would be seen as a further drain on the availability of specialists to teach mathematics.

4. Heads of department recognised that mathematicians saw computer studies teaching experience as a means of gaining promotion. The increasing number of references to computing in advertisements for mathematics posts would seem to confirm this view.

5. Specific examples were quoted of specialist mathematicians who now taught no mathematics but had a full teaching load in computing.

From the findings of the LEA study it would appear that the growth of computer studies has, in terms of manpower, been staffed at the expense of mathematics departments, and usually with the more effective and innovative teachers subject to the mismatch.

Initial training

At PGCE level is it possible that more could be done to persuade arts students to follow computer studies as a subsidiary subject. At present the majority of students opting for computer studies are mathematicians. Table 2 shows the main subject specialisms of students on the PGCE course at the University of Newcastle upon Tyne who take computing as their second method subject.

Table 2 Main subject specialisms of PGCE computing students, University of Newcastle upon Tyne

Subject	Year					
	1979	1980	1981	1982	1983	Total
Mathematics	10	7	6	12	10	45
Biology	1	0	0	2	0	3
Chemistry	0	3	0	0	0	3
Geography	0	1	1	1	2	5
Physics	0	0	3	1	3	7
Total	11	11	10	16	15	63

Many mathematics specialists undergoing initial training opt for subsidiary computing because it seems to be the 'obvious' choice which will improve career prospects. Often these students lack confidence in their ability to teach computer studies effectively, however, partly because they lack background knowledge and also because they find difficulty in keeping up to date with developments. The techniques required to teach social implications and historical details, for example, differ greatly from the skills required for effective mathematics teaching, and this presents the student with further difficulties. Yet mathematicians who are prepared to offer computing are more successful in finding employment. Some mathematics students are now finding that they are required to spend up to 50 per cent of their teaching time in the probationary year engaged in the teaching of computer studies.

A recent survey of PGCE main mathematics students at six English universities investigated their views on the teaching of computing. Of 134 students who replied, fifty (37 per cent) were following subsidiary method courses in computing. Five of the 134 students who replied were graduates in mathematics/computing, two in computer science, one in physics/computing and one operational research/computing. The replies are summarised in Table 3. The following comments made by the students about computer studies teaching give some indication of the level of feeling

Table 3 Views of PCGE main maths students at six universities

	Training to teach CS	Not training to teach CS
Would you prefer a post where you taught computer studies as well as maths?		
Yes	21	12
No	11	54
Undecided	18	18
Would you accept a post where you taught computer studies as well as maths?		
Yes	39	34
No	4	24
Undecided	7	26
No. of students expressing confidence at teaching computer studies at the levels shown:		
CSE	40	42
O level	33	29
A level	7	6

As mathematicians are usually the best qualified members of staff to teach computer studies, I feel that they should teach it.

It's very sensible to use mathematics staff, as they've usually had some experience with computers.

It's wrong that it's automatically expected that mathematics staff are capable, and willing, to teach computer studies. Much of the course seems more suited to teachers of arts subjects.

In my opinion teachers should teach maths as a main subject and then use the microcomputer as an aid to teach that subject. It's a rather unhappy state of affairs, because maths teachers are being lured into computing, feeling that there are better career prospects.

Computer studies is often taught badly because only maths staff teach it. For the theory part, maths staff seem to teach it in a mathematical way, without proper discussion.

Computer studies should not weaken the mathematics department, nor should it be seen by children as a 'maths' subject. Teachers of other subjects should be encouraged to teach it too.

A good maths teacher may well make a good computer studies teacher, but there is more to computer studies than a purely mathematical viewpoint. If mathematicians are the only ones who teach computing, this will make the subject unnecessarily narrow.

In the long term computer studies should become a subject in its own right, taught by specialist teachers. The current trend of staffing computing with maths staff is a contributory factor to the shortage of maths teachers. In particular it's often the more able and enthusiastic maths teachers who are taken, causing a larger drain on maths teaching resources than that shown on a purely numerical basis.

I love maths but I don't find computing very interesting. However, I feel that in order to increase my chances of obtaining a maths post I will have to learn to teach computing.

It does appear that some mathematics students, having experienced computer studies course work, and having taught the subject on teaching practice, are beginning to have reservations about computer studies. A number of students commented that they would much prefer to use their programming expertise in the mathematics lesson than in a separate subject. It would be interesting to investigate whether teachers of other main subjects who take computing as subsidiary share these views. It is certain that at present our initial training of computer studies teachers is not meeting the needs of schools, either in terms of manpower levels or in providing the requisite level of expertise. Wellington (1983) supports the view that there is an urgent need to train computing specialists:

[The Alvey Report] identifies the urgent need for an adequate supply, in both quantity and quality, of properly trained graduates to teach computer studies as a school subject . . . But first, who are the people teaching computing as a subject in its own right? The number of graduates actually trained to teach computer studies is ridiculously low, in spite of the fact that, as a school subject, it is now firmly established.

The present approach to the staffiing of computer studies has several weaknesses. Firstly, the diversion of mathematicians to computing must cease, as it is having a serious effect on the teaching of mathematics, which remains very much a shortage subject at secondary level. It also seems unreasonable to burden heads of mathematics or their deputies with overall responsibility for computing. The role of the head of mathematics is important and demanding, and it is not reasonable to expect him or her to take on this extra load. Maintenance and management of equipment is time-consuming, and it is therefore important that computing departments are given technical support.

If the manpower position is to be resolved, a major retraining programme is essential. With rolls falling, teachers of some subjects could be retrained: this had been done effectively in two schools in the case study LEA, where a geographer and a PE teacher had undergone a retraining programme and now had overall responsibility for computing in their respective schools. It is therefore important that LEAs have a policy on computer education across the authority so that the necessary resources and in-service training are provided for teachers. Forward planning may in time ease the pressure on mathematics departments. Our schools need computing departments staffed by specialists who are able to take a broader view of what is meant by computer education. Until this comes about, the effective use of the microcomputer in mathematics lessons will remain a rare occurrence.

References

Butterworth, I (1983), *Staffing for Curriculum Needs*. London: NFER and Nelson.
Department of Education and Science, Committee of Inquiry into the Teaching of Mathematics (1982), *Mathematics Counts* (the Cockcroft Report). London: HMSO.
Fletcher, T. J. (1983), *Microcomputers and Mathematics in Schools*, a discussion paper. London: Department of Education and Science.
Straker, N. (1983), 'Who teaches Computer Studies?' *Times Educational Supplement*, 4 November.
— (1984) 'Where have all the maths teachers gone?' *Education*, 18 May.
Strong, R. W. (1984), 'Pressure of numbers', *Times Educational Supplement*, 2 March.
Thorne, M. (1983), 'Basic ambiguities', *Times Educational Supplement*, 4 November.
Wellington, J. (1983), 'Computing in the curriculum', *Times Educational Supplement*, 4 November.

11. Micro-PROLOG and classroom historical research

RICHARD ENNALS

As part of the Local Studies course at Bishop Wand Church of England Secondary School in Sunbury, use is made in class of trade directories for the village from the nineteenth century, in conjuction with other local records such as the census records of particular streets. Part of the course is spent on fieldwork, with walks round the village looking at old buildings, studying inscriptions on tombstones in the churchyard, and comparing the present-day village with what is shown on a series of maps dating back two hundred years, written accounts since Saxon times, and archaeolgical evidence.

The work described here involved the use of the trade directories for 1826, 1840, 1860, 1865, 1872 and 1876. Each separate directory was represented as a PROLOG data base, and as many as three directories could be loaded into memory at once for simultaneous interrogation. Most classroom activity focused on the computer interrogation of the directories for 1826, 1840 and 1867, with all the directories also available in printed form, laid out on large cards for each pair of students. The computer used was a Corona, an IBM PC-compatible portable microcomputer, using a version of micro-PROLOG that addressed 128K of memory.

Use of the trade directories without a computer

Below are the questions usually set to the students when the directories are used without computer assistance. They indicate the general approach taken on the course.[1]

1826
1 Who was the vicar?

2 Which house is Sunbury is described as 'The late possessed by the Earl Pomfret'?

3 How many times a day were letters sent to London?

4 How may public houses were there in Sunbury in 1826?

5 What would a tallow chandler sell? Why was his job important?

6 Make a list of the jobs and services carried out in Sunbury.

7 How frequent was the coach service to London from Sunbury?

1840

1 Louisa Ruff seems to have more than one job. One is postmistress. What are the others?

2 What does a farrier do? Why would this job be important in nineteenth-century Sunbury?

3 Is the coach service to London more or less frequent than it was in 1826?

4 Who would you to to if you wanted a straw hat made in 1840?

5 How many fishmongers were there in Sunbury?

6 Who was the governor of the workhouse?

1867

1 What new invention has arrived in Sunbury by 1867? How do you know?

2 How could you travel to London in 1867? How frequent was the service?

1872 and 1876

Look at the addresses given for William Allen, baker, Charles Collett and William Thomas Collins and Son. What appears to have happened between 1872 and 1876?

From 1801 a census taken of everyone living in England and Wales. The trade directory entries give the details for 1821, 1831 and 1861: 1,700, 1,863 and 2,332 respectively. Draw a graph to show these figures.

Using trade directories with the computer

The class, of twenty-five twelve-year-olds, had no previous experience of either the computer or the trade directories. Seven directories, each lengthy and printed in small type, could not usefully be interrogated without some familiarity with the historical context, apart from what had been acquired on the course to date. An examination was made of the directory for 1826. Initial questions asked, for written answer and discussion, were:

1 What five things do you notice about the directory?

There were a variety of responses, such as: 'not many people', 'not many different jobs', 'the people have been split up and classified', 'for each person we have the name and group', 'for some people we have an address', 'for some people we have a particular job, or trade', 'not many women mentioned', 'some of the jobs are not known today'.

2 What different jobs did people do in 1826 in Sunbury?

Students first wrote down the different jobs by hand, then saw how the same question could be asked of the computer, and answered fully in seconds. In PROLOG the question was:

which (x: x lived 1826 and x trade y)

3 What were the names of the pubs and their landlords in 1826?

Again the answers could be found by hand from this, the smallest of the directories. In PROLOG the question was

which (x y: x lived 1826 and
              x trade (publican) and
              x address y)

The idea was thus introduced that the historian needs to decide what question to ask of his evidence. If he has only a small amount of evidence to deal with, he can probably search for the answer perfectly well himself. If, however, he is faced by a large amount of evidence, such as the seven trade directories, he may be well advised to take advantage of the assistance of the computer, which can carry out the search according to his description of the information that is required. A good historian knows what questions to ask, and what to do with the answers. He must not be the slave of the evidence in front of him. Trade directories were produced for a particular purpose, and much information about the village would not have been explicitly included. The task is to reconstruct something of life in nineteenth-century Sunbury, including relating it to other knowledge we have at a local, regional or national level concerning the same period.

There followed the suggestion of a wide range of possible research projects, to be carried out by individuals or small groups over the two weeks of the course unit. Suggestions included: following an individual, such as John Baker, Dr Seaton; following a family, such as Baker, Lambert, Broxholm, Bolt; following a trade, such as saddler, wheelwright, publican, baker, beer retailer; following institutions, such as workhouse, private asylum, schools and academies; following addresses, such as Sunbury Lodge, and noting the increasingly full addresses given, including street names; comparisons of, for example, 1826 and 1840, 1840 and 1867; evidence of the role of women; evidence of changing means of transport; evidence of increasing education; evidence of family businesses; evidence of the influence of the river and the country; changing trades and occupations.

The method to be used by the students was that they should choose a topic, and write their chosen title, followed by a short outline of what they wanted to investigate. They should then write down in English the first question they wanted to ask the computer, bearing in mind the kind of information that is contained in a trade directory. The teacher then put the question to the computer in PROLOG, and the student made a note of the answer. He could then ask further questions arising from what he had learnt, following the same procedure. He also noted what information he would require from other sources, such as further details about particular families which might be found from the local census records. In some cases the student had relevant knowledge from other sources, and this should be incorporated in the written notes. For example, a student investigating the Baker family knew of a house in Sunbury with an inscription saying that Robert Eldridge Baker (mentioned in the directories) had built it.

After the investigation, the work could be presented in a number of forms, all drawing on the research, such as a diary (perhaps of Miss Broxholm, the doctor's daughter), a biography (perhaps of the grocer who became a schoolmaster), a family history (Baker by name and baker by trade), a comparative study, a play, a traveller's tale (told by a visitor at the Flower Pot inn), a guide to Sunbury, accompanied by maps.

The PROLOG representations of the trade directories

A sentence in PROLOG is used to represent the information for each person. For example, to take the first entry in the 1826 directory, concerning Wm Barclay esq.:

lived-1826 ((Barclay Wm esq) (Upper Halliford) gandc ())

and for the publican of the Flower Pot inn:

lived-1826 ((Long John) (Flower Pot) pub (publican))

As observed by the students, we have information about a person's name, address, grouping and trade. In the above sentences the information is presented in that order. In some cases no specific address or trade is given, in which cases I have used '()', denoting the empty list of information. There are rules to give us access to these items of information:

    x address y if lived-1826 (x y z X)
    x class Gentry-and-Clergy if lived-1826 (x y gandc z)
    x trade y if lived-1826 (x z X y)
    x lived 1826 if lived-1826 (x y z X)

The same approach is used for the 1840 and 1867, etc., directories, the only change being in the number of the year used in the sentences and rules.

Sample student questions in English and PROLOG

Which people were wheelwrights by trade, and when did they live?
which (x y: x trade (wheelwright) and x listed y)

Which people were publicans, and which pubs did they run?
which (x y: x trade (publican) and x address y)

Which people are mentioned in the directories for 1826, 1840 and 1867?
which (x: x lived 1826 and x lived 1840 and x lived 1867)

What were the addresses of the gentry and clergy who described themselves as 'esq'? (This question arose with a student who was concerned to find out who had carriages, and where they lived.)
which (x y: x class Gentry-and-Clergy and esq ON x and x address y)

What was the total number of people mentioned in 1867?
which (x: y isall (z:z lived 1867) and y length x)

What were all the different jobs done by people, not counting those with no stated job?
which (x: y trade x and not x EQ())

What different trades did people have in 1840?
which (x y: x lived 1840 and x trade y)

Whose trade included being a baker, and when did they live?
which (x y z: x trade y and baker ON y and x lived z)

Give me information on everybody's trade and class.
which (x y z: x class y and x trade z)

Give me the address and trade of people whose address was stated to be in Sunbury in 1840.

which (x y z: x lived 1840 and x address y and Sunbry ON y and x trade z)

Tell me about the trades of individuals who lived in 1826 and 1840.
which (x y : x lived 1826 and x lived 1840 and x trade y)

Tell me about the names, addresses and trades of members of the Bishop family, and when they lived. (The same question was asked about the Burchetts, the Lamberts, the Bakers, the Gileses and the Middletons.)
which (x y z X: x trade y and Bishop ON x and x address z and x lived X)

What work did women do? (We defined new rules that would pick out cases of people described as 'Miss' or '(Mrs)' in the directories.)
x female-doing y if x trade y and Miss ON x
x female-doing y if x trade and (Mrs) ON x
We can now ask:
which (x y: x female-doing y)

What did the 'professional people' do?
which (x y: x class Professional-Person and x trade y)

What were the names and addresses of the hairdressers, and in what years? (The same form of question was asked about grocers, plumbers, smiths and saddlers.)
which (x y z X: x trade y and hairdresser ON y and x address z and x lived X)

Questions raised by the students but not answerable from the trade directories alone, with or without PROLOG

What is the origin of the name Burchett (or Bishop)?

Were the different people with the same surname Bishop (or Baker, etc.) related and, if so, in what way?

How were inns in the nineteenth century different from today? (Students noted that the Flower Pot was a staging post for coaches, and that seats could be booked at the other inns.)

When did the centre of activity in Sunbury really move from the riverside to the other end of Green Street, nearer the railway, and why?

What happened to people who were too young or too poor to be mentioned in the trade directories?

What happened in the private asylum at Halliford House, and at the workhouse on Sunbury Common?

How did life in Sunbury change with the coming of the railway?

What did the gentry do all the time, as they had no stated trades?

What was going on in all the different schools and academies that are mentioned? Should we be surprised that one of them was run by a former grocer?

Why was insurance suddenly such a significant form of employment in Sunbury?

To what extent was Sunbury a country village at the beginning of the century? How did this change?

What problems did the police sergeant have to deal with?

Why did stationmasters but not engine drivers live in Sunbury, or would the directory not mention employees, or people who travelled to work?

Where had the gentry got their money?

Was there increasing military activity in the area? (We read of a military college, and a number of naval officers are local residents.)

What was the extent of the influence of the Church in Sunbury? Were the people named in the directories elsewhere recorded as church members? Did support for particular churches come from particular social classes or trades? Was the Church particularly active in educational, social or mission work?

What do we know about local and parliamentary politics in the area? Who had the right to vote?

Were most people in Sunbury born in the area, or had many moved in for work or other reasons?

What were the working conditions like in the local shops and businesses? Did many local people work as servants for the local gentry?

Conclusion

The research reports produced by our twelve-year-old historical researchers will not necessarily be long or of lasting quality. The pupils will, however, have experienced something of what it is to ask historical questions, and to make sense of the answers. There can be some division of labour with the computer: the student decides what question to ask, and the computer performs the mechanical search for the answers. The ease of representing information in PROLOG in a form that remains comprehensible, and the capacity to ask and answer numerous different questions, make it possible for each individual or group to pursue a separate line of inquiry if they wish. New facts and rules can be added at will: sections of trade directories could be interrogated together with census data or entries from the parish register.

In the lessons described above questions were asked in English by the students, and translated into PROLOG by the teacher. More sophisticated query systems are under development that will assist the user to formulate a query using a series of menus to clarify the structure and vocabulary of the data base. Already developed, though demanding of computer memory space, are systems that will automatically translate questions from English into PROLOG and answer them efficiently.

We should note the methodological context of historical research through asking questions. Questions to a PROLOG data base can be answered only from the closed world of information that it contains. Many questions will require further information if they are to be answered. The computer can have a powerful motivating effect on research and learning: hypotheses can be treated and improved, new areas of interest can be brought to light. There will always be more questions than answers, and the computer can help clarify which lines of inquiry are worth pursuing at a given time.

Note
1 Largely developed by Mrs Elizabeth Hossain.

References
Collingwood, R. G. (1946), *The Idea of History*. London: Oxford University Press.
Ennals, J. R. (1984), *Beginning Micro-Prolog* (second, revised edition). London: Ellis Horwood and Heinemann.
Ennals, J. R. (1985), *Artificial Intelligence: Applications to Logical and Historical Research*. London: Ellis Horwood.
Labbett, B. D. C. (1977), *The Local History Classroom Project, 1975/1977*. London: Council for Educational Technology.
Macfarlane, A. (1977), *Reconstructing Historical Communities – Records of an English Village, Earls Colne, 1400–1750*. London: Cambridge University Press.

12. CAL IN THE GEOGRAPHY CLASSROOM

PATRICK WIEGAND

Geography teaching in the 1970s became increasingly characterised by a number of features that were to ensure a warm welcome for the arrival of microcomputers in the 1980s. The examination boards, for example, responded to the so-called 'quantitative revolution', whereby description had been replaced by the scientific method, measurement, model and theory-building. Fieldwork came to consist typically of projects involving the collection of data followed by some sort of statistical test in order to prove or disprove hypotheses. Particularly popular, for example, was (and remains) the use of correlation coefficients to measure the relationship between, say, stream discharge and other characteristics of the stream channel, such as slope or the amount of suspended sediment present. Statistical techniques, though, were not confined to physical geography. By 1980 all A level geographers knew (or ought to have known) how to collect and process data to demonstrate that there is usually a relationship between such variables as building height or rateable value and distance away from a city centre. Neither were such techniques confined to A level geography. The first chapter of book 3 of the Oxford Geography Project (one of the most successful geography textbook series of the 1970s), designed for third-year pupils, begins with correlation.

Changes were also taking place in the style of teaching adopted by many geography teachers. The Schools Council curriculum development projects – Geography for the Young School Leaver, Geography 14–18 (and, later, Geography 16–19) – did much to evangelise the use of resource and inquiry-based learning. Individual projects became a popular part of the assessment pattern at sixteen-plus. Of particular importance in teaching technique was the widespread acceptance – if not actual implementation – of games and simulations (Walford, 1969). By 1980 most schoolchildren following a course in geography would have engaged in some decision-making activitiy designed to teach them about which crops to plant, where to build the railway or where to search for North Sea oil. Most self-respecting geography textbooks included a game of some sort.

By the early 1980s, when microcomputers and geography software were appearing in schools in quantity, even 'newer' geographies were threatening to overtake the 'new' school geography of the '70s (Wiegand and Orrell, 1982). They included geography seen not as a science but as a personal response to landscape and environment (see, for example, Fien, 1983). Such *humanistic* geography encourages pupils to explore their own feelings and attitudes towards place and to clarify those values. *Radical* geographers, on the other hand, question the supposed neutrality of scientific geography and attempt to focus attention on issues of welfare and spatial injustice (Peet, 1978). Nevertheless, despite these later trends, it is probably true to say that most school geography by the early 1980s was still essentially positivist in character. It was this that made the prospect of using the microcomputer particularly appealing. Much of the early software took the form of statistical packages or computer versions of existing games or simulations. In addition there was the prospect, for this information-heavy subject, of storing large quantities of data that could be sorted, analysed and retrieved at will.

Some early enthusiasts had used computers before 1980. These tended to be mainframe or mini-computers used either via a telephone modem unit or as batch processing. Indeed, the handbook which for several years was to be the only guide to computing in school geography was written when hardly any schools had access to a micro (Shepherd *et al.*, 1980). The background to the expansion of microcomputing is well known, particularly with respect to government involvement via the Department of Industry scheme which provided cash to match money raised locally for the purchase of approved hardware and the Micro-electronics Education Programme, which was responsible for information, training and curriculum development. However, amidst the general euphoria and optimism of this growth spurt there were, in some quarters, signs of cynicism and disquiet. Shepherd (1983) has drawn attention to some of them in the context of geography. In a subject already battered by rapid change

CAL in the geography classroom   139

during the previous decade the prospect for many older teachers of further alienation, this time by new technology, was daunting. In addition many of the claims made by computing enthusiasts were seen to be exaggerated, for much of the software available did not appear to exploit the potential of the hardware fully. Despite a growing literature of the 'How to do it' or 'How I did it' type (e.g. Stevens, 1980; Watson, 1982) there had been little observation and evaluation of the ways in which the microcomputer had been used in the geography classroom. A great deal of time and money had been invested in fitting a micro into every school, and yet, as Wragg (quoted in Kent, 1982) characteristically asked, 'Will anyone take the trouble to see whether teachers are favourably disposed to it, properly trained to exploit its potential, have enough software; will anyone inquire how it is actually used or even whether the wretched machine is ever unwrapped?'

It was in this spirit that a number of observations were made of lessons where a microcomputer was used to teach geography. The initial aim was modest: to document and reflect on the use being made of micros by geography teachers in this early period of their use. Specifically the aim was to discover the ways in which teachers managed the micro in their classrooms and the ways in which pupils participated in learning.

One of the problems of classroom studies is the range of theoretical and methodological approaches available (Hammersley, 1982). Classroom research in computer-assisted learning has been largely within the positivist tradition. Classroom interaction analysis, (for example, the SCAN notation), has been used in the context of mathematics by Beeby et al. (1979), and teacher styles have been compared in geography computing lessons by Hassell (1982). However, at a time when computing in geography was not widespread the present writer was content merely to report the results of coarse-grained observations. Twelve lessons were observed and the lessons were recorded on videotape. It was thereby possible to record not only pupil and teacher talk but also the computer monitor screen. Videotape was also used because of its potential for pre-service and in-service training at a time when the demand for such training was running high (Adams and Biddle, 1970).

Computer-using teachers were identified by questionnaire. It was sent to heads of geography departments in the MEP region of West and North Yorkshire every Easter from 1981 to 1983. Its distribution was carried out in collaboration with colleagues at the Universities of Bristol and London; the results of this wider survey are reported elsewhere (Hall *et al.*, 1984). The responses of Yorkshire teachers were not dissimilar to those of teachers from Avon and parts of Greater London. During the period 1981–83 the hardware, software and teachers expertise grew rapidly. In Yorkshire the average number of micros in secondary schools increased from fewer than two in 1981 to seven in 1983. By Easter 1984 it was estimated that there were twelve per school. The period was also marked by an increase in geography software. Although there were early initiatives in software development (notably by the Huntington II project and the National Development Programme in Computer Assisted Learning) and an early appearance in some texts of computer data (e.g. Cole, 1972) the first programs to have a wide impact on geography teachers were those produced by the Schools Council Computers in the Geography Curriculum project team. These programs, published in 1979, included *Demog*, *Mill* and *Farm* – still the most popular geography programs in Yorkshire in 1983. By then, compared with more recently published software, they were beginning to look dated. The cost of commercial software, the time needed to evaluate it and the time lag before it could be fitted into the appropriate point in the syllabus often led to a substantial delay between publication and classroom use.

A breakdown of the number of lessons by age of pupils, size of class and name of program is shown in Table 1. Each lesson was observed within the normal teaching sequence, i.e. there were no special demonstration lessons. Note that in Leeds and Bradford entry to a high school is usually at the age of thirteen. Lessons with eleven-to-thirteen year-olds may therefore be under-represented in the sample. All the teachers observed had approximately ten years' teaching experience, and most were heads of department. All had taught at least six previous lessons using microcomputers. They represented a selection of the most computer-experienced geography teachers in the region.

The programs used in the lessons observed were representative of the geography programs used throughout the region (Hall *et al.*, 1984). These were mainly from the Schools Council Computers in the Geography Curriculum material described above (Watson, 1979).

Demog was the most popular among geographers in the region. It allows the user to make population projections, using data provided or

Table 1 Summary of lessons observed

Program used	Age of pupils	No. of pupils	No. of micros available	Type of lesson organisation
Demog	13–14	16	8[a]	Groups (static)
Demog	13–14	25	2	Groups (cafeteria)
Demog	13–14	26	1	Whole class (plus contestants)
Demog	16–17	10	1	Whole class (plus contestants)
Mill	14–15	32	2	Groups (cafeteria)
Mill	13–14	24	4	Groups (static)
Mill	13–14	24	1	Groups (cafeteria)
Farm	13–14	16	3	Groups (cafeteria)
Farm	13–14	25	3	Groups (cafeteria)
Gravity	16–17	12	1	Whole class (plus contestants)
Hurkle	11–12	27	1	Whole class (plus contestants)
Network	17–18	12	2	Groups (cafeteria)

a Mini-computer with eight terminals.

new data. Birth and death rates can be altered, and the program will display population pyramids as well as numbers. Pupils learn the long-term effects of changes in birth and death rates. *Mill* is a game where windmills are located on an imaginary island. The program calculates the cost of locating at each possible site in terms of transport costs, power supply, etc. Pupils learn which factors affect the location of mills.

Farm is a simulation where fields on one of three farms are planted with a choice of crops. The return on each field is then determined by weather conditions typical of the region in which the farm is located. Pupils learn the most appropriate combination of crops for each region and the effect of chance weather conditions on income. *Gravity* (Stevens and Blandford, n.d.) is a program based on Huff's probability model of consumer behaviour and calculates the probability of consumers at a number of locations visiting a choice of market centres. The user must input distances from consumer locations to market centres, the size of market centres and a value for the exponent in the gravity formula. *Network* is a program, developed by the teacher who was being observed, which calculates connectivity and accessibility indices for a given transport network. *Hurkle* (Shepherd, n.d.) is a grid-reference practice game. An imaginary animal is hiding in a square-shaped region. Its location must be found by guessing co-ordinates. Clues (e.g. 'Go north-west') are given to the player, who must find the 'hurkle' in a specified number of guesses.

In all the lessons observed, the hardware was in use throughout the lesson. The children seemed aware that it was a special event – a treat or a privilege. The lessons were frequently not held in the geography room at all but in the TV room or laboratory. In their introduction to the lessons the teachers usually made some comment about 'the wonders of modern technology' and 'I hope there isn't a power failure'. They gave explicit justifications for using the micro in geography, commenting on its advantage as a rapid calculator enabling pupils to see the results of calculations they either couldn't do or that would take them too long to do by hand:

> *Teacher*. Right, now, it says, 'Calculation in progress.' A series of noughts appear, that's quite OK. The calculation is in progress. The computer is working it out. The computers are very fast. The amount of time that computer is taking to work out your little exercise tells you it's a very complex one. It would take you several weeks to work it out by hand. So we have a short pause while we wait. [Third year, *Mill*]

In one lesson (*Gravity*) pupils had difficulty with the simple arithmetic necessary to tot up distances to enter into the program. The gravity model calculations would clearly have posed problems by hand. Although reference was made to the potential of the computer in individual projects, its sole reported advantage as a learning aid was as a fast calculator.

However, despite the speed of calculation the use of the micro was seen as potentially hazardous. Strict teacher control was deemed necessary, and teacher instruction had to be closely followed:

> *Teacher*. Now, bring your chairs so that you can sit round. The first thing is that a lot of these computers, they reckon they're child-proof and idiot-proof, but this isn't so. It's very easy with a lot of these programs to what's called 'crash' a program, that is, by pressing the wrong thing at the wrong time to completely wipe out what we're trying to do, so for the moment don't touch anything unless I've told you its OK to touch it. OK? [Third year, *Mill*]

Successful operation of the micro was seen as requiring acquired skill. The pupils would need help at first. The whole structure of the lesson was generally devised to enable the teacher to provide that help. However, once the teacher had provided the necessary guidance, pupils would be able to proceed on their own.

> *Teacher*. Most of the questions it wants you to answer will be very clear. It will say, 'Type YES', and 'Type NO', or whatever it wants you to do. The first time you use the computer, the first time each group comes out, I'll

stand with you, and I'll just have a quick check so that you know what you're doing. If you get an answer that doesn't make sense – it tells you something like – 'Type mismatch' or 'Syntax error' and it just won't do anything – just tell me, and I'll come and I'll sort it out for you – OK? Most of the time you should find that you can run it without me having to be standing over you. The second time round, I won't stand over you. It's exactly the same sort of process, and you should be able to do it without any help. Is that clear? [Third year, *Mill*]

Many of the teacher comments about the micro betray teacher anxiety or anticipate anxiety on the part of the pupil:

> *Teacher.* For those of you that haven't used the machine before, I'll hover, so you feel safe. [Third year, *Network*]

Three main styles of using the micro were observed. In *whole class teaching* the teachers usually used one micro in conjunction with several TV monitors. The computer provided the focus for the lesson and the teachers talked the class through the program, using a question-and-answer approach. For example in a lesson using the program *Hurkle* the teacher led class discussion about which would be the best guess at a grid reference to locate the 'hurkle'.

Whole-class teaching was usually adopted by teachers with only one micro. In addition to 'normal' participation by pupils in these lessons all the teachers observed who were teaching to the whole class invited one pupil or a succession of pupils to type at the keyboard. This is a version of the popular teaching technique of asking a pupil to come to the front of the class and demonstrate a point on the blackboard. As operating the computer was seen as a special treat, and as the pupils' involvement was similar to that of the TV quiz or game show in which members of the audience are selected for participation, the term *contestant* seems appropriate. Pupils take it in turns to (e.g.) find the 'hurkle' within the prescribed number of guesses or locate the mill more cheaply than the previous contestant. Audience participation in the form of calling out advice, etc., is often at a high level.

Teachers justified the use of contestants in lessons on grounds of increased motivation and as an opportunity (albeit limited) to provide 'hands on' experience for at least a few pupils. In the example that follows the pupil at the front does not participate on his own behalf as a *contestant*, making his own decisions, but acts as a more passive *button presser*, entering responses decided on by the teacher and the rest of the class. Apart from a cynical view of ministerial responsibility, note how the teacher refers to the computer's role in the lesson and how he acts as an intermediary, encouraging the class to give instructions to the button presser.

Teacher. What you need is some nice calculator to help you work out how many people there might be, and some intelligent guesswork. Well, we've got the calculator here, that's why we're in this room, with the computer, and we've got a program which quite conveniently does all the calculations for us. So we're just using this as a calculator today. Now, who's going to be the Minister of the Day?
Pupil. (inaudible).
Teacher. Well, you've just volunteered yourself, Martin, Come on. (*Pupil goes to front.*) There are three TV screens, so people at the back can look at that one by the window. (*The program has been set up in advance, and the only word on the screen says 'Country?'*) Right, what's the country?
Pupil. India.
Teacher. Right, would you like to type in *India*? 'I'. (*Pupil enters* India.) There's a button marked 'Return', would you like to press that? Top right. Yes. OK. [. . .] What's the year of the information?
Pupil. 1971.
Teacher. 1971. Numbers are on the top [of the keyboard]. (*Pupil types* 1971.) Press 'Return'. Good. [. . .] Someone tell him, from the sheet, what the population was? [. . .]
Teacher. Right. We want to know the percentage increase, don't we? Now look at those figures. Where does it say 'Increase' or 'Decrease'? Someone help him. (*To boy at front.*) You just be a button-presser for the time being. You just do as you're told. If you're a Minister you get all these civil servants to do the work for you, don't you? (*To class.*) Right, come on, then, civil servants. Where are we told this information? Right, go on . . .
[Fourth year, *Demog*]

The second observed style of micro management was in *group work*. Teachers preferred to adopt this style when there were sufficient micros available. 'Groups' of one or two pupils were thought ideal by the teachers, but in one lesson groups of six were noted. In this case there was little participation by the 'second row' of pupils seated at the computer. Pupils often acted as committee members in groups, each with a teacher-given role. Groups were often in competition with each other – for example, to find the lowest cost site for windmills. Sometimes this competition was deliberately planned by the teacher.

The third management style was the *cafeteria classroom*. Groups of pupils were given a number of tasks, only one of which involved using the micro. In one lesson each group acted as a firm of planning consultants writing a report on the best location for windmills. Their submission had to include maps of the island, a report on local conditions and the operation of the mills, and the results of their trial runs of the program. When the micro was free the groups proceeded to the computing task.

While they were waiting they carried out the non-computing tasks. However, time was a major preoccupation for teachers using micros in this way. The computer had usually been booked in advance and was therefore available for that lesson only. All the computing had to be accomplished within the lesson.

> *Teacher.* Right, while you're waiting your turn each group has got some tasks to get on with. If you haven't selected the sites . . . then you have a priority. You must get your site selections made, because if you haven't got your site selected when it's your turn to use the computer you lose your turn, and we'll fit you in again at the end – if we can, but we may not be able to. We're on a tight time schedule. [Third year, *Mill*]

The limited access to the hardware seemed more critical than any shortage in the number of micros. Teachers were as anxious to complete the computing tasks in the one lesson regardless of whether there was one or eight micros present.

The most striking feature of all the lessons was the strong element of teacher directiveness. In the following extract the teacher instructs pupils to alter birth or death rates in a carefully prescribed way. He then demonstrates the results of such changes later, using the figures and pyramids each group has produced.

> *Teacher.* Our chief aim is to set up a number of scenarios for population development in Third World countries, and in England and Wales. Group 1, for example, are looking at what happens when birth rates fall slightly. . . . Group 1, I'd like you to go on raising your death rate after 2020, so if you can remember to do that . . . [Third year, *Demog*]

Later in the same lesson the teacher refers to a hand-out in which the basic structure of the pupils' tasks is set out.

> *Teacher* (*referring to hand-out*). I've listed at the bottom of the first page the years for which you'll carry out the projection. [Third year, *Demog*]

Significantly, every lesson observed made use of a work sheet. The central task in most lessons was to complete this hand-out. Pupils worked through prepared stages, completed boxes, entered scores and drew graphs that had been scaled for them. The results of the pupils' computing were then collated by the teacher and used in whole-class demonstration and exposition. This style of teaching has its parallels in the hypothesis-testing, data-collection style of fieldwork in which each pupil or group collects, for example, central business district land use data and then pools results for a class map.

In all the lessons observed the teachers kept a tight rein on the learning that was taking place. In the following lesson the teacher is not only leading the pupils' thinking but at the end puts a brake on their curiosity to discover what will happen if the population were to continue growing at the same rate. The pupils in this group have been examining the population growth of a less developed country. They have followed the teacher's instructions and he is now telling them what they should have noticed.

Pupil (referring to print-out). That's impossible!
Teacher. Two hundred and what?
Pupil. Two hundred and ninety-three million.
Teacher. No, it's not impossible, it's quite likely, isn't it?
Pupil. Oh!
Teacher. Can you explain why it's two hundred and ninety-three million?
Puil. It's sort of exponential growth . . . it sort of doubles . . . or whatever . . . and keeps going on like that, just adding on . . .
Teacher. Any why is it growing so sharply?
Pupil. Well, its still got a very high birth rate but – er – a very low death rate, because now . . .
Teacher. . . . . relatively low, yes—?
Pupil. . . . . they've got medical care.
Teacher. And what about the pyramid shape? Any changes? What about the sides of the thing?
Pupil. Well it's just sort of . . .
Teacher. They're concave, aren't they?
Pupil. Yes.
Teacher. Yes, so you've probably seen very little change actually, have you?
Pupil. No, not as far as actual *shape* is concerned. It's just that the numbers get bigger.
Teacher. Right, so exponential growth, then, and a wide difference between birth and death rates, tends to produce that sort of pyramid, and that remains stable, doesn't it, over the years? [. . .]
Well, you're almost ready to start graphing, aren't you? The figures that you'll graph are those at the top here – you see? – in each case. The graph paper has been scaled for you, ready for that. OK?

Later, another group are projecting their population figures.

Teacher. How far have you got?
Pupil 1. Two thousand and twenty.
Teacher. Yes, do 2040 and 2080. Finish when you've done 2080.
Pupil 2. We might be able to do 2090.
Teacher. No, finish when you've done 2080 and then construct your graph.
[Third year, *Demog 2*]

Although this last section of the transcript could be interpreted as the teacher leading pupils away from unnecessary repetition of a task, it seemed at the time that the discovery of a pattern of demographic change was being stifled.

It is possible to speculate as to why the lessons observed were so strongly teacher-directed. Firstly, no examination was made of non-computing lessons taught by the teachers concerned. It is possible that the twelve lessons described here represent their normal styles rather than ones deliberately adopted in response to computing lessons. Secondly, shortage of time may have disposed them towards a strongly teacher-controlled framework to the lessons.

A third reason may have been the desire to achieve a satisfactory result, especially in the presence of an observer. This feeling may have been heightened by *relative* inexperience in the use of micros in the classroom. It may be that a safe, conservative or traditional style of teaching is a necessary stage that has to be passed through when faced with an innovation.

All the teachers maintained strict control of the learning that was taking place in their lessons. Little independent exploration of the program was permitted. Little opportunity was given for the pupils to ask 'What would happen if . . .' questions of the programs, yet the application of such questions has been regarded as a strength of computer-assisted learning. No evidence was seen of 'serendipity learning' (Rushby, 1979). All the teachers wanted their pupils to have maximum access to the hardware, yet, paradoxically, they exhibited a strong desire to control what pupils learned from that access. In Shepherd's 'gatekeeper' model the gatekeeping nature of the teacher was in respect of access to hardware:

> 'In the 'gatekeeper' model, the teacher sees the computer as his personal preserve, and any access by students is carefully controlled and monitored. Sometimes a teacher is unwilling to allow students any direct access to the computer. This clearly denies students any opportunity of learning by their own experiments'. [Shepherd *et al.* (1980), p. 116]

What is proposed here, however, is that teachers were acting as gatekeepers to pupils' personal interaction with the programs. In every case the teachers were the initiators. There was little partnership in learning.

Interviews before and after the lessons also confirmed Hartley and Bostrom's (1982) findings that 'teachers did not break new ground, but used the programs to consolidate principles they have covered immediately before'. The computing lessons were invariably at the *end* of a teaching sequence. The programs reinforced learning or provided revision rather than initiating new learning or prompting enquiry.

It is clear that computer-assisted learning in geography is still at an early stage of its development. Classroom implementation of CAL is closely related to the nature of the programs available. New types of program may imply new styles of classroom use. Most of the programs in the lesson described above were simulations. The more recent growth, however, has been in short 'utility' programs and in database packages. It remains to be seen to what extent the balance of control and initiative will move from teacher to pupil and program.

References

Adams, R. S., and Biddle, B. J. (1970) *Realities of Teaching: Explorations with Videotape.* New York: Holt and Rinehart.

Beeby, T., Burkhardt, H., and Fraser, R. (1979), *Systematic Classroom Analysis Notation.* University of Birmingham: Shell Centre for Mathematical Education.

Cole, J. P. (1975), *Situations in Human Geography.* Oxford: Blackwell.

Fien, J. (1983), 'Humanistic Geography', in J. Hunkle (ed.), *Geographical Education: Reflection and Action.* Oxford: Oxford University Press.

Hall, D., Kent, W. A., and Wiegand, P. A. (1985), 'Computer-assisted learning in geography: the state of the art, in *Teaching Geography*, 10(2), January.

Hall, D., Kent, W. A., and Wiegand, P. A. (1982), 'Geography teaching and computers', in *Teaching Geography*, 7(3), January.

Hammersley, K. (1982), 'The sociology of classrooms', in A. Hartnett (ed.), *The Social Sciences in Educational Studies: a Selective Guide to the Literature.* London: Heinemann.

Hartley, J. R., and Bostrom, K. (1982), 'An evaluation of Micro-CAL in schools', *International Journal of Man—Machine Studies*, 17, pp. 127–141.

Hassell, D. (1982), 'Teacher style and CAL in Geography'. MA dissertation, University of London: Institute of Education.

Kent, W. A. (1982), 'The challenge of the microcomputer' in Graves, N. J., *Geography in Education Now*, Beford Way Papers, No. 13. London: University of London Institute of Education.

Peet, R. (1978), *Radical Geography.* London: Methuen.

Rushby, N. J. (1979), *An Introduction to Educational Computing*. London: Croom Helm.

Shepherd, I. D. H. (n.d.), *Hunt the Hurkle: Handbook*. Middlesex Polytechnic: Computers in Geography Study Group.

— (1983), 'The agony and the ecstasy – reflections on the microcomputer and geography teaching', in Kent, W. A. (ed.), *Geography Teaching and the Micro*. London: Longman.

Shepherd, I. D. H., Cooper, Z. A., and Walker, D. R. F. (1980), *Computer Assisted Learning in Geography*. London: Council for Educational Technology with the Geographical Association.

Stevens, W. (1980), 'Using computers in geography teaching', *Classroom Geographer*, April, pp. 3–11.

Stevens, W. M., and Blandford, J. A. (n.d.), *Gravity Model Handbook: How a Computer can be Used with a Gravity Model in Geographical Fieldwork*. Hatfield: Advisory Unit for Computer Based Education.

Walford, R. (1969), *Games in Geography*. London: Longman.

Watson, D. (ed.) (1979), *Computers in the Geography Curriculum*. London: Schools Council/Longman.

Watson, M. (1982), 'The place of CAL in developing the geography curriculum', in Wiegand and Orrell (1982).

Wiegand, P., and Orrell, K. (eds.) (1982), *New Leads in Geographical Education*. Sheffield: Geographical Association.

13. Word-processing in school

BOB CAMPBELL

This chapter in a book on the uses of microcomputers in the classroom concerns their role as word-processors. It focuses on the word-processing activities of a group of pupils completing their final year of primary education and presents and discusses examples of their work. Gosling (1978) wrote:

> the productivity of everybody who works with words should immeasurably increase – not in regard to volume, for that would be a mixed blessing – but rather in the ease with which the text can be revised, reviewed, corrected and updated. The quality of writing will no longer be limited by the fatigue of its improvement.

When these words were written they were seen to hold significance only for those whose profession is the creation and manipulation of written text. This is no longer so. Word-processing, as a tool, has much to offer *all* who write as part of their daily activity, and among these I count schoolchildren. One of the most important educational applications of the new information technology is word processing, yet it has received scant attention compared with such activities as the study of computers, computer programming and computer-assisted learning. Although much far-reaching development work in communications technology is being undertaken, it must be recognised that, for the foreseeable future, the printed word will remain the dominant educational medium and the act of writing will retain its central importance as an educational activity.

But it also must be recognised that the physical act of writing is, for many children, such a laborious and time-consuming endeavour that they seldom progress to develop, practise and improve the further

Word-processing in schools   151

skills of correction, revision and refinement of their writing. However, by using the word-processor rather than a pen, a pupil has access to a range of powerful editing facilities requiring little effort to operate. The removal of the chore of having to write and rewrite text encourages experimentaton with language. The content of the text and the ideas which are looking for expression become the focus of the exercise, and not the physical act of writing nor even the spelling, grammar nor punctuation. These details can be tackled once the pupil is satisfied with the language. Word-processors can help pupils to explore language and to create more interesting and more effective text.

While this is not the place to provide a detailed account of word-processing systems or word-processing, it is perhaps appropriate to provide an outline description of the systems available to schools. There are three main systems: (1) a machine specially made for word-processing (a dedicated word-processor), (2) a special program on a mainframe computer, (3) a special program on a microcomputer.

It would be rare to find a school with a dedicated word-processor or relying on a link to a mainframe computer to provide a word-processing capability. By contrast, and thanks largely to the Department of Trade and Industry financing schemes and MEP support structures, there can be few, if any, schools without at least one microcomputer either in action or on order. It is a simple matter to equip a microcomputer with a software package to enable word-processing to be tackled. This may be provided on tape, disc or ROM chip. Such word-processing packages are available for the two makes of computer most widely used in schools. For the RML 380Z and 480Z, *WordStar*,[1] though costly, is a powerful package. *Word*[2] is considerably cheaper but much less powerful. Users of the BBC microcomputer have a wide range of packages to choose from. Perhaps only three are likely to become established in schools; *Wordwise*,[3] which is claimed to be the most popular of all the BBC word-processing packages, *View*,[4] the official Acorn word-processor, and *Edword*,[5] which has been developed specifically for educational use. The following remarks refer to such software packages.

At the simplest level of description, a word-processing package turns a microcompter into a device which is similar to an electronic typewriter, allowing the correction and amendment of text before it is printed. Text is entered at the computer keyboard and displayed on the screen so that it can be viewed as entered before it is printed on paper. Word-processing packages have two sets of features, one to edit text and one to allow the organisation of the format in which the text will appear. Coupled with this is the facility to save text on tape or disc store and call it up at a later date. This enables work to be left and returned to without the need for retyping, and also the merging of text from different 'electronic' files to make composite documents.

Text entry is considerably simplified by automatic end-of-line determination and 'wrap round', which prevents the splitting of words. Entry errors can be corrected immediately by an electronic 'rubber'. Because the text is held electronically and can be scanned quickly, it is a simple matter to correct, delete or insert characters, words, lines, sentences, paragraphs or even whole sections of text. Similarly, selected sections of text can be moved to new positions. Furthermore the whole text can be searched for given characters or words so that they may be replaced, either selectively or even automatically. The availabilty of such facilities promotes the extensive review and editing of text. There is no need for every edit or redraft to be a rewriting task. Material can be worked and reworked until the writer is completely satisfied with the result.

To get the most out of any word-processor one must have a printer to produce 'hard copy' output. It is in the design of the format of this output that the second set of word-processing facilities provides powerful tools. It is possible to set values for parameters such as line length, page length and line spacing. Because these can be so readily changed and the effects previewed on the screen prior to printing, experimentation with format is encouraged. Centring of headings, tabulation and indentation, justification of margins, spacing of sections of text, page numbers, running headings and footings are also easily dealt with by simple commands. A number of printers allow the control of print size and style from within a word-processing package, even enabling a variety of sizes and styles to be used in the same section of a document. Blocks of text may be transposed, reordered, replaced and reformatted several times in the course of an electronic edit, just as they could on paper using the 'cut and paste' technique. The advantages which the word-processor confers are those of speed and convenience. There is thus considerable potential for encouraging the creation of work which is not only 'good' when judged on linguistic or literary criteria but which is also 'good' in terms of its presentation.

Some of the early experiences of word-processing in schools are recorded by Adams,[6] who reports on a project initiated in some secondary schools in Birmingham. The project concentrated on the use of word-processing in typewriting classes and awareness courses for students, in the creation and production of curriculum material by staff and in school administration. When the machines were not being used for such purposes they were given over to computer studies students. While some secondary schools may still see their priorities for word-processing continuing in such directions it is unlikely that primary schools will. There is already some evidence[7] to suggest that primary schools will harness word-processing power for creative writing.

Advice on the selection and use of word-processing equipment in schools has come from the Council for Educational Technology (CET, 1982). They suggest a range of educational roles for word processing in schools. One suggestion is for developing awareness of the application of micro-electronics, another for improving office administration. A set of suggestions are offered for classroom applications. Prominent among them is the suggestion that the development of pupils' communication skills can be aided by using word-processors to express ideas in writing in the form of reports, stories, poems and plays.

So much for the rhetoric. What is the reality? Can pupils learn how to use a word processor, and if so how long does it take and what can they do with it? Above all, what influences does it have on their learning?

The word-processing activities described below were completed over two short periods of time. The initial work was one of several activities in a series spanning a single-day 'awareness course' organised for a local primary school and run on three separate occasions for each of their three junior-4 classes. These computer days were set up in school to provide both pupils and their teachers with experience of a range of computer-based activities. Because they were planned with and partly staffed by the class teachers, they were seen as staff development exercises as well as curriculum enrichment experiences. Pupils worked in groups of two or three to move round each of five 'stations' at which there were simple programs to key in and run, various computer-assisted learning exercises to try, a data base to interrogate and a word-processor to use. A variety of computers were brought into school to resource the stations, the word-processing activity being based on a Commodore Pet and

Wordpro[8] package. The equipment was set up and the software loaded for use prior to the arrival of the pupils. Beside each station there was a set of written instructions for the particular activity. Pupils were asked to organise their own day but to do all the activities. They moved from activity to activity, and were free to return to any activity as they wished. Staff provided support as required. At the time the school had no computer of its own: for most pupils it was their first experience with computers and, for all, their first experience of word-processing. While some spent more time at the word-processor than others, no group spent more than ninety minutes at the activity.

The results of the word-processing activity are regarded as most encouraging. This is particularly so when one considers that the pupils had little keyboard familiarity and that the word-processing package they were using was not designed for children and, by current standards, is far from 'user-friendly'. All pupils were able to enter text, edit it and print it out on paper. Because all were keen to see a 'hard copy' of their work at an early opportunity the text grew as individuals added their contribution to an entry. All experimented with different formats. Most graduated to saving their text on disc and recalling it for editing, extending or reformatting. What was most noticeable was the confidence with which they handled the word-processor and the rapidity with which they mastered the various commands and functions. This was much aided by a great deal of pupil–pupil interaction and discussion and a willingness to engage in co-operative learning.

It was not the intention that pupils should produce lengthy pieces of prose but rather that they should gain some idea of the capabilities of the word-processor. Examples of the word-processing are given in Figs. 1, 2 and 3. These are taken from the disc files created by the pupils.

Rachel, Glyn and Chris (Fig. 1) chose to write about a recent trip to London. Although it took them a little time to realise that both upper and lower-case letters could be printed, they tried different layouts and revised their text to improve the spelling and grammar. A rather different approach was taken by Colin and Philip (Fig. 2). They used the word-processor to edit and extend their fantasy story. As their highly personalised account develops it becomes more like a sports report, and it is perhaps significant that the boys chose a presentation format not unlike that of a newspaper, with a narrow column width and a justified right margin. The final example of pupil word-

(a)

```
I WENT ON A TRIP
TO LONDON.  WE
WENT TO THE
NATIONAL HISTORY
MUSEUM AND THE
TOWEROF
LONDON,THERE WE
SAW THE CROWN
JEWELS.  WE
ALSO SAW THE
RAVENS
by  Rachel
Girling.Glyn
Jones. Chris
Wedgwood.
```

(b)

```
I WENT ON A TRIP TO LONDON.  WE
WENT TO THE NATIONAL HISTORY MUSEUM
AND THE TOWEROF LONDON,THERE WE SAW
THE CROWN JEWELS.  WE ALSO SAW THE
RAVENS.
by Rachel Girling. Glyn Jones.
Chris Wedgwood.
```

(c)

```
I WENT ON A TRIP TO LONDON.  WE WENT TO THE NATIONAL HISTOR
MUSEUM AND THE TOWEROF LONDON,THERE WE SAW THE CROWN JEWELS
 WE
ALSO SAW THE RAVENS.
by Rachel Girling. Glyn Jones.
Chris Wedgwood.
```

(d)

```
We went on a trip to London.  We went to the Natural Histor
Museum and the tower of London where we saw the Crown
Jewels.  We also saw the ravens.

by
Rachel Girling, Glyn Jones and Chris Wedgwood
```

Fig. 1

156   Teachers, computers and the classroom

(a)

```
Once   upon   a   time   there were two
boys called Phillip and Colin.  One
day thet were very excited  because
they    were    chosen  to  play  for
Liverpool in the
European
Cup Final for the first time
```

(b)

```
Once upon a  time  there  were   two
boys called Phillip and Colin.   One
day  they were very excited because
they   were   chosen   to   play   for
Liverpool in the European Cup Final
for   the   first time.  In the first
half there was a lot ofend  to   end
football.   Then   after   16 minutes
they scored a goal.  At  half   time
the   score was 1.0 to them.  In the
second half Phillip   ran   down   the
left  wing   crossed  it   and   Colin
headed it into the back of the   net
which  made  it   1.1.   Soon  after
Colin put a good  through  ball   to
Phillip   who   took   it   round   the
keeper and scored.  So at   the   end
of   the   match the score was 2.1 to
Liverpool.
```

Fig. 2

processing (Fig. 3) is another personalised piece produced by a group
of girls who not only used the simpler text editing capabilities of the
word-processor but were able to centre text and to use the tabulation
to give their work a professional appearance.

The experience of the computer days indicated that pupils had no
fears of using a word-processor and could quickly control a variety of
its functions, producing acceptable and novel work in a short space of

time. Even those who said that they did not 'enjoy' writing indicated their enthusiasm for word-processing and confidently exhibited their print-outs. What was clear, however, was that the experience which had been provided was too limited and too concentrated. Pupils were just getting into the way of using the word-processor and exploring its capabilities when their colleagues were encouraging them to move on to a new activity. In addition, and perhaps most important, it was noted that while the pupils readily accepted the use of the word-processor as an editing tool for the correction of errors in typing, spelling or grammar, they did not necessarily see it as an aid to revision, restructuring or rewriting. Plans were thus made for a word-processing activity which it was hoped would overcome such difficulties. In order to encourage the 'revision' of work, it was agreed that there should be some tangible outcome of the exercise and that it should take the form of a simple, pupil-produced news sheet. The pupils were to have responsibility for the collection of information, keyboard entry, editing and compilation.

Following the initial series of computer days, the school acquired its own BBC system and developed a programme of computer familiarity for its senior pupils. It thus seemed sensible to base any

THE RALLY

One day Jenny and Beth woke up to find their Mum
on the phone talking to Mrs Nicholson about the
netball rally. When she put the phone down she
told us that we were going to be in it. We were
very excited and quickly put our clothes on. When
we eventually arrived at Naburn School the rally
was just starting. We were second to play
Burnholme School. We had a victory against this
School with a score of 13-0. In fact we beat all
the other Schools which included:

                    Fulford   School
                    Stamford   "
                    Dringhouses   "
                    St Georges   "
                    Derwent   "

The trophy was awarded to us by the Lord Mayor.

THE END

Fig. 3

further word-processing activity on the use of this machine, with which, it could be assumed, the pupils were becoming familiar. The choice of word-processor was similarly straightforward, as only one (*Wordwise*) was available in more than one machine. This choice was perhaps not quite as pragnatic as it may seem, as *Wordwise* has gained wide acceptance as a simple-to-use yet powerful word-processing system, and as such was being considered for purchase by the school.

Whereas all the senior pupils had been directly engaged in the initial word-processing activity, this was not possible for the 'news sheet' exercise. Consequently teams of three pupils were drawn from each of the three senior classes. Three half-day word-processing sessions were organised so that each team would have complete access to a BBC microcomputer system, with *Wordwise*, a disc drive and a printer. In the first session, pupils followed a set of work-sheet instructions for activities designed to illustrate the capabilities of the word-processor and to allow them to become familiar with its command set. The other two sessions were arranged a week after the initial one. During the intervening week pupils were asked to collect information to turn into their 'stories' for the news sheet. These sessions, which were organised on consecutive days, were thus devoted to entering, editing and revising text and putting it into a format suitable for a news sheet.

Nothing emerged during the first 'familiarity' session to cast doubt on the previous conclusion that pupils approached the word-processor confidently and learned quickly. Again it was noted how well they co-operated and assisted each other to use the technology. Even though three pupils were sharing a machine and each team was composed of boys and girls, a 'fair shares' system developed, so that each pupil took it in turn to work at the keyboard while the other two looked on, offered advice and discussed any problems which arose.

When the pupils arrived for the second session of word-processing some had rough drafts, some notes and some only ideas from which to compose their news stories. Regardless of this, they set about their task enthusiastically. The 'copy' varied in quality, quantity and to some extent content. Because a few memorable events had recently taken place in school, these received coverage from more than one pupil. The teams were not instructed how to organise, edit or revise their work, but each team was asked to discuss and review each piece it produced. As before, the word-processor was used to assist the correction of spelling and grammatical errors. Only occasionally did pupils change the form of the text, move pieces of text from one section to another or enter additional text.

Figure 4 provides examples of text taken from the disc files of one team which illustrate how a story was edited and formatted. Twelve pieces developed in this way during the two word-processing sessions. To accommodate them within a news sheet of manageable proportions, they were photo-reduced from A4 to A5, reprinted and arranged to form an eight-page booklet (see Fig. 5 for a sample page). The 'tangible product' of the exercise was presented by the pupils with great pride and regarded by all as a considerable achievement in a short period of time. This was seen as particularly important for one pupil, who was selected to take part in the hope that it would encourage him to overcome the problems he was experiencing with reading and writing.

An unexpected outcome was the series of word-processor 'doodles' (Fig. 6) which the pupils produced to illustrate the news sheet. These arose from one girl's experiments with different ways of presenting her name. The expertise was soon shared, and the 'doodles' resulted. Such a use of the word-processor well illustrates the views of Papert (1981) that the child should and can control the computer, and not the computer the child. Papert also believes that the word processor is important to children as a writing instrument, as it offers them opportunities to operate more like adults in relation to their writing. Although the experiences reported here are limited, they indicate that a word-processor does place children in control and that they can respond in a positive way. What is less certain is that pupils in this position can see and consider other than spelling, grammar or typing errors and use capabilities of the word-processor other than the simple editing and formatting facilities. Thus it may be that if we wish pupils to use a word-processor to 'revise' their writing in the sense of improving its language, form, style or clarity, then we may need to produce schemes of work that encourage it. Perhaps we need also to take note of developments in the technology. We already have word-processors with built-in spelling checkers, and in the pipeline are electronic dictionaries and thesauruses, so that some of the writing 'chores' may be taken care of with little effort, so leaving energy for creativity.

But what did the pupils think of it all? In addition to the 'feedback' picked up during the word-processing activities, their reactions were gauged by means of a short questionnaire designed to determine whether they thought the experience had been of benefit and whether they considered that word-processing could become part of normal classroom activities. All agreed that the experience had been worthwhile but that three to a machine was too many. They did not admit to any great difficulty with the use of the machine, but rather with the 'setting', where aspects such as margins, spaces between words and after punctuation marks, and the use of capital letters, featured in comments. They found things like storing work on disc and printing out very easy, and saw them as particular advantages allowing the use of the word-processor for 'project work' and 'good copy'. No pupil saw the word processor as a tool for the revision of writing in terms other than the correction of errors. All agreed that it would be useful to have a word-processor in school, but they also recognised the limitations of a single machine and the management problems it would create for the teacher.

What has been given little mention to date is keyboarding. Clearly, to use the current generation of word processors effectively, the user must be able to enter text at the keyboard efficiently. Text entry which depends on a 'hunt and peck' technique is slow and inefficient. If we wish children to use word-processors (and indeed computers) there is much to be said for teaching correct keyboarding techniques so that all ten fingers are used and eyes can be kept on the screen rather than the keys. Indeed, it can be argued that introducing word-processing without teaching keyboarding is inappropriate. The experiences reported here would tend to support that view: although pupils were able to use the word-processor to some advantage, much time was spent on text entry. In their questionnaire responses pupils mentioned initial difficulty in locating the keys and though they stated that 'typing was easy' a few were clearly frustrated by slowness at the keyboard (both their own and their colleagues), and one wrote that the hardest thing about word-processing was 'typing the work in quickly'. Had pupils been quicker and more accurate at this, they would perhaps have been able to use the technology to greater advantage. However, there may seem little reason to teach keyboarding skills unless pupils see a purpose in it. With young children there is the added problem of small hands and large QWERTY keyboards. The Microwriter Quinkey is one example of a device designed to combat it but this too has its limitations. Although there are other ways of data entry into a computer via character recognition systems, light pens and bar code readers, and we hear of

SPORTSDAY

On Thursday 28th June Heslington school had their Sportsday.
The first race was the 1st year girls sprint. The winner of
the race was Julie Edison for Lloyd putting them into the
lead. Lloyd were'nt so lucky in the 1st yaer boys sprint
because Hesketh came first and second. In the 2nd year
girls sprint Lloyd came third after Ruth Fletcher who came
first for Yarburgh and Heskeths Jillian Girling came second.
In the 2nd year boys flat race Robert Jones for Lloyd came
first Mark Daniel and Steven England came second and third
for Lloyd. In the other races it was very close as Yarburgh
wre only a few points in the lead.
   In the relays Lloyd won 3 firsts 1 second and the other
four teams in lloyd came third , that was'nt enuogh to beat
Yarburgh. The final score was:

                    Yarburgh 103 points
                    Lloyd   93\ points
                    Hesketh   91\ points

(b)

SPORTSDAY

On Thursday 28th June 1984 Heslington school had their
Sportsday. The first race was the 1st year girls sprint.
The winner of the race was Julie Edison for Lloyd putting
them into the lead. Lloyd weren't so lucky in the 1st year
boys sprint because Hesketh came first and second. In the
2nd year girls sprint Lloyd came third. Ruth Fletcher came
first for Yarburgh and Heskeths Jillian Girling came second.
In the 2nd year boys flat race Robert Jones of Lloyd came
first, Mark Daniel and Steven England also of Lloyd came
second and third. In the other races it was very close as
Yarburgh were only a few points in the lead. In the relays
Lloyd won 3 firsts, 1 second and four thirds. That wasn't
enough to beat Yarburgh. The final score was:

                    Yarburgh 103   points,
                    Lloyd   93.5 points,
                    Hesketh   91.5 points.

Peter Jones

Fig. 4

(c)

SPORTSDAY

On Thursday 28th June 1984
Heslington school had their
Sportsday. The first race was
the 1st year girls sprint.
The winner of the race was
Julie Edison for Lloyd putting
them into the lead. Lloyd
weren't so lucky in the 1st
year boys sprint because
Hesketh came first and second.
 In the 2nd year girls sprint
Lloyd came third. Ruth
Fletcher came first for
Yarburgh and Heskeths Jillian
Girling came second. In the
2nd year boys flat race Robert
Jones of Lloyd came first,
Mark Daniel and Steven England
also of Lloyd came second and
third. In the other races it
was very close as Yarburgh
were only a few points in the
lead. In the relays Lloyd won
3 firsts, 1 second and four
thirds. That wasn't enough
to beat Yarburgh. The final
score was:

Yarburgh	103	points,
Lloyd	93.5	points,
Hesketh	91.5	points.

Peter Jones

The Mediaeval Spectacular

On Saturday 16th June 1984 a lot of the third and fourth years took part in the York Mediaeval Spectacular. Our mother helpers took us to The Minster. As our group arrived everyone clapped and cheered. When Mrs Brudenell arrived everyone cheered extra loudly. We were in the procession that went right round The Minster. As soon as we had gone in we sat down to watch some enormous puppets. The first was Winter. Winter was a cone shaped creature. A man came on three-metre stilts. He threw some torn up paper and kept running around blowing a whistle that was meant to be wind. Spring was a lady in purple. Two ladies had to pull her feet along. Inside you could see a man carrying the body and head. Two more ladies moved the arms. Summer was The Great Green Giant. He was green and worked the same as Spring. Next came the Dance of Death. A monster came on with an ugly face. He had only one hand and he hit people with it. Then came Hell. He was the tallest puppet of all. He had a red and white striped face and red horns. He wore a long red robe. As soon as that was over we went into the north aisle to perform our country dancing. The first dance was Patacake Polka. Next we moved into our places for Circassian Circle. We then did two other dances. When we had finished we rushed over to the South Transcept to do our maypole dancing. Then we were allowed to do what we liked.

Emma Frost

Fig. 5

THE BARBECUE

On Saturday 30th June, Heslington School held a Barbecue. There were fancy dress competitions in which many children dressed up like different animals and people. The infants had to dress up as monsters, the first and second years as birds and finally the third and fourth years as T.V. personalities. There were hamburgers, hot dogs, sweets and crisps on sale. Also there was a special machine that was making badges. You could design your own badge or you could cut a picture from a book for your badge. There was an air bed on which many children enjoyed themselves by bouncing on it. While all of this and the fancy dress netball was happening, a band played music. Some parents had offered to dress up and take part in the fancy dress netball. The game itself had no rules apart from one: to score you had to throw a ball through the net at the top of the netball post. When play began it was more like a rugby match with the ever present referee Mrs Nicholson assuring fair play. The fancy dress netball was fast and furious and it was a shame when the game ended. Mr Emery and Mr Ulett were running a treasure hunt around Heslington village, the winner of which won a box of chocolates. Also some children took part in country and maypole dancing. Balloons were also on sale. Inside Mr Riley was running a "Connect Four" competition, the winner of which also won a box of chocolates. It was a very enjoyable evening.

Michael Edison

```
                  chim            chim
                  neys            neys
            roofroofroofroofroofroofroof
            roofroofroofroofroofroofroofro
            ofroofroofroofroofroofroofroofro
            ofroofroofroofroofroofroofroofroof
            wallwallwallwallwallwallwallwall
            wallwindowwallwallwindowwwall
            wallwindowwallwallwindowwall
  %%%       wallwindowwallwallwindowwall
 %%%%%      wallwindowwallwallwindowwall
 %%%%%      wallwindowwallwallwindowwall
  %%%       wallwindowwallwallwindowwall
buzzzzz     wallwalldoordoordoorwallwall
buzzzzzzz   wallwalldoordoordoorwallwall
buzzzzzzz   wallwalldoordoordoorwallwall
buzzzzz     wallwalldoordoordoorwallwall
            wallwalldoordoordoorwallwall
            wallwalldoordoordoorwallwall
            wallwalldoordoordoorwallwall
            wallwalldoordoordoorwallwall
            wallwalldoordoordoorwallwall
            wallwalldoordoordoorwallwall

    z   a   g   z   a   g   z   a   g   z
     izgizgizgizgizgizg
     g   z   a   g   z   a   g   z   a

    z   a   g   z   a   g   z   a   g   z
     izgizgizgizgizgizgi
     g   z   a   g   z   a   g   z   a   g
```

Fig. 6

speech recognition systems under development, there seems little doubt that for the immediate future, regardless of its limitations, text entry to word-processors will be by QWERTY keyboard. A recent report Jones (1984) indicates that keyboarding will be one of the most important job skills for school-leavers. Furthermore the same report recognises that experience of word-processing is needed by both boys and girls, and not just by those looking towards a career in computing or in an office support role.

Word-processors are powerful tools of the business and commercial world, and their use is increasing with all whose professional life centres on the written word. Their use in education can be justified on a number of grounds – to create awareness of their importance, to encourage the development of related skills which have a high currency in terms of future employment, and, most important, to use them as tools for creativity. If this latter is to be achieved, there is a need for pupils to develop keyboarding skills and for teachers to devise ways of encouraging them to see text revision as more than the correction of errors in spelling, punctuation or grammar.

Word-processing in schools   165

Notes

1 *WordStar* is a disc-based word processor for CP/M-based microcomputers. It is available from Research Machines, Mill Street, Oxford.

2 *Word* is a simple disc-based word-processor for the RML 380Z microcomputer, designed to be used for introducing the concepts of word-processing. It is available from the Advisory Unit for Computer Based Education, Hatfield, Hertfordshire.

3 *Wordwise* is a ROM-based word-processor for the BBC microcomputer. It is available from Computer Concepts, Hertfordshire.

4 *View* is the 'official' Acorn ROM-based word-processor for the BBC microcomputer. It is available from Vector Marketing, Wellington, Northants.

5 *EdWord* is a ROM-based word-processor for the BBC microcomputer. It was developed for educational use through the Micro-electronics Education Programme and is supplied with teaching materials. It is available from Clwyd Technics, Rhydywyn, Clwyd, Wales.

6 See 'Word-processing in schools', *Computer Education*, 43 (February 1983), pp. 24–5, which contains extracts from Adams, (1982), (now out of print).

7 See, for example, Bryan (1983) and Heaney (1984).

8 *Wordpro* is a disc-based word-processor for the Commodore Pet range of microcomputers. It is available from Supersoft, Wealdstone, Harrow.

9 The Microwriter Quinkey is keyboard which can be held and operated with one hand. It has only six keys, which when pressed in particular combinations code for the seventy-two different characters and functions of the BBC microcomputer. Further details are available from Microwriter, 31 Southapton Row, London.

References

Adams, B. (1982), *Word Processing in Schools*. University of Birmingham: Faculty of Education.

Bryan, P. (1983), 'Word Wise', in *Times Educational Supplement*, 2 November.

Council for Educational Technology (1982), *Word-processing Systems in Education: a Guide to the Applications and Selection of Suitable Equipment*, USPEC 32b, available from the CET, 3 Devonshire Street, London W1N 2BA.

Gosling, W. (1978), *Microcircuits, Society and Education*. London: Council for Educational Technology.

Heaney, P. (1984), 'More Like Adults', in *Times Educational Supplement*, 25 May.

Jones, Ann Glyn (1984), *Job Skills in the Computer Age*, report prepared for Devonshire County Council and the University of Exeter, available from the Publications Office, University of Exeter, Exeter EX4 4QJ.

Papert, S. (1981), *Mindstorms: Children, Computers and Powerful Ideas*. Brighton: Harvester Press.

14. Computers and pupil records

CHRISTOPHER W. BUTCHER

What constitutes a pupil record system – the school roll, the individual files held by pastoral staff, the records of external agencies that contribute to the welfare of pupils, a mark book, the awareness/ mental records of individual teachers about pupils seen daily in the school environment? Rushby (1979) defines a student record as:

> Collections of information about students and groups of students, including such things as: the courses they are studying, the history of their studies, their results in diagnostic tests and examinations, background information about their learning preferences, aspirations and problems, comment made about them by their teachers, home address, date of birth and so on.

His incomplete proposals can be distilled down into three main categories:

1 Personal record (name, address, date of birth, factors affecting welfare, aspirations, etc.).
2 Educational record – outline (subjects studied, group membership, etc.).
3 Educational record – detailed (marks, tests, teacher comment, pupil response, parental contact, etc.).

The former two categories have particular relevance to the management of the institution, whilst the latter is of specific importance to the management of learning. Whether it is possible and/or desirable to encompass these categories within one record system is one theme of this chapter.

Maddison (1982) emphasises that the fundamental administrative item in a school is the school roll. Albeit obvious, this reminder does give a starting point. Within an institution that does not use a computer for administrative purposes some, if not all, of the records mentioned earlier already exist. If a computer-based system is to be proposed or implemented it is necessary to consider the extent of such a system or, perhaps more important, decide the restrictions to be placed on the development. Accepting that the roll is fundamental to any system, this chapter considers the justification, or otherwise, for extending a simple name-recording system to encompass other necessary administrative functions. It considers the validity, feasibility and desirability of computer-based administration (CBA), and discusses guidelines for any developments in terms of the file fields included, access limitations and security implications. The need for records (a contentious issue in itself) will not, generally, be questioned.

Desirability

The desirability of computer systems in school administration can be considered from three standpoints: firstly the advantage of improving efficiency – saving time, providing more relevant and updated information; secondly, the disadvantage of possible misuse of a system – security and file content; lastly the case of use and essential functions required of a system need consideration.

Management in any organisation has to make decisions, be they long-term policy plans or short-term contingencies. Whatever the organisation, whatever the decision, it is essential that reliable and relevant information is available and that such data are presented in a concise and meaningful manner. Schools as organisations are increasing in both size and complexity, and this results in the managers being more remote from, and hence less knowledgable of, the individuals within the organisation. Decisions affecting members of the organisation have to be made upon the basis of records of information gathered by others. Whilst a manual record system would be unlikely to satisfy the managers' needs in these circumstances – the time and staff are not available constantly to update, sort and present the required information – a computer system, given appropriate software, could fulfil the requirements. Jenkins and Melhuish (1983) comment that a manual system of school administration 'does not lend itself easily to flexibility, either in terms of solving a given problem, or in its application to allied situations.' They also note that paper or card stored files are rarely, if ever, duplicated, and question the outcome if such files were to be lost or destroyed. A school in Worcestershire faced just that problem in 1983 when a fire destroyed the administration block and all the records it contained. The school had to canvass the area to 'find' its pupils. Copying computer-held information, as all commercial software houses are only too aware, is extremely easy. Similarly a box or two of floppy discs – the duplicate records – are unlikely to cause too great a strain on storage space.

These points alone give sufficient justification for considering the use of computers for storing school records. The SCAMP (1982) project notes the importance of relevant and reliable information for use in schools, and extends the need to local, regional and national authorities. Similarly Bird (1982) concludes, after a survey of schools using microcomputer-based administration (MCBA) systems, that the availability of extra and more accurate information is one of the advantages that such systems offer. He notes a second desirable feature of MCBA: that time, hence money, is saved and efficiency increased. The desirable aspects of time saving and increased efficiency can be emphasised by considering a particular example. Whilst the application described is not, at present, part of a integrated system it is envisaged that it should be an option to such, and so able to access information from the central files.

Sixteen-plus practical assessment: *Assess* (1983)

The current Cambridge University/West Midlands Examination Board sixteen-plus chemistry examination involves a school assessment component. It requires the teacher to assess 'practical skills' in terms of six 'qualities'. These qualities (A-F) should be 'scored on several occasions during the course' and the marks averaged for each pupil for each quality. (Typical records for two pupils part way through the course are given as Fig. 1(a).) For each quality the candidates are to be placed in rank order, based upon the averaged marks, and assigned a position between 20 (top) and 1 (bottom) – Fig. 1(b). For each pupil the positions are totalled and a final rank order determined – Fig. 1(c). It is this information that the examination board requires. The time required to process raw marks by hand or by calculator is considerable. The computer takes a little under ten minutes to process and print. Whilst the time saving is

ARROW VALE HIGH SCHOOL   CHEMISTRY 16+

ASSESSMENT RECORD FOR   CATHERINE C

	A	B	C	D	E	F
1	18	18	18	18	17	9
2	16	16	14	16	18	9
3	17	16	13	14	18	7
4	18	13	14	1	13	9
5	9	15	0	15	0	8
6	0	0	0	0	0	0
7	0	0	0	0	0	0
8	0	0	0	0	0	0
9	0	0	0	0	0	0
10	0	0	0	0	0	0

POSITION   20   1
OVERALL RANK IN SET:- 20   20   20   19   20   10

CHEMISTRY 16+   ARROW VALE HIGH SCHOOL

ASSESSMENT RECORD FOR   MARK M

	A	B	C	D	E	F
1	14	14	14	14	14	8
2	14	14	14	14	14	9
3	16	16	16	16	16	9
4	16	16	15	15	15	7
5	0	17	0	16	0	9
6	0	0	0	17	0	0
7	0	0	0	0	0	0
8	0	0	0	0	0	0
9	0	0	0	0	0	0
10	0	0	0	0	0	0

POSITION   19
OVERALL RANK IN SET:- 19   19   2   19   20   19   9

(a)

170   Teachers, computers and the classroom

ATTRIBUTE=-C

NAME	AVE	POS	NAME	POS
CATHERINE C	14.8	20	CHRIS C	17
MARK M	14.8	19	MARK M	19
WENDY W	12.7	18	CATHERINE C	20
CHRIS C	8	17	WENDY W	18

ATTRIBUTE=-D

NAME	AVE	POS	NAME	POS
MARK M	15.3	20	CHRIS C	17
CATHERINE C	13	19	MARK M	20
WENDY W	12.7	18	CATHERINE C	19
CHRIS C	7.3	17	WENDY W	18

(b)

ARROW VALE HIGH SCHOOL   CHEMISTRY 16+

Surname-Forename	Assessment of Quality						Total	Rank in Set	Assessment
	A	B	C	D	E	F	/110		2TEST
CHRIS C	17	17	17	17	17	7	92	4	
MARK M	19	19	19	20	19	9	105	2	
CATHERINE C	20	20	20	19	20	10	109	1	
WENDY W	18	18	18	18	18	8	98	3	

(c)

Fig. 1

(*a*) DO YOU WISH TO   CODE

     PREPARE A FILE   1

     SAVE A FILE   2

     LOAD A FILE   3

     INPUT MARKS   4

     PRINT OUT   5

     EDIT A FILE   6

     WORK ON ANOTHER FILE   7

     EXIT   8

(*b*) DO YOU WISH TO   CODE

     ADD A PUPIL   1

     DELETE A NAME   2

     AMEND A NAME   3

     AMEND AN ENTRY   4

     RENAME THIS FILE   5

     ERASE THIS FILE   6

     RETURN TO MAIN MENU   7

(*c*) DO YOU WISH TO   CODE

     PRINT OUT A PUPILS RECORD   1

     PRINT OUT ALL RECORDS   2

     PRINT OUT ORDERED LISTS   3

     PRINT OUT A SUMMARY   4

     RETURN TO MAIN MENU   5

Fig. 2   (*a*) Main menu. (*b*) Print menu (main menu option 5). (*c*) Edit menu (main menu option 6).

172   Teachers, computers and the classroom

obvious, a second advantage may not be so apparent. The 'number crunching' can be quickly and conveniently done at any time, and so pupils can be advised as to weaknesses within their assessments on an exact, comparative basis. Prior to *Assess* the calculations were done just once, at the end of the course, when feedback to pupils was irrelevant. The software is menu-driven, (Fig. 2), thus allowing alterations, deletions and additions as appropriate.

The justifications offered by SCAMP (1982) members, Jenkins and Melhuish (1983) and Bird (1982) are emphasised and reiterated throughout the literature. Dooley (1983), discussing the organisation of an efficient system, concludes, 'the advantages to be gained from computers [in school administration] far outweigh the initial hardships'. Cowie (1976) waxes lyrical on the advantages of computer-stored option choices, and asks non-users: 'Do you really do all that sorting by hand?' Piddock (1975), discussing the use of computers to assist with school administration, with special reference to DES Form 7, notes, 'given the existence of such a data file [machine-readable pupil information file], the operation of the program to produce the information required for the completion of Form 7 is a trivial matter'. Gallagher (1982) reinforces the point that the computer can release valuable time from tedious list sorting, concluding that 'teachers have better things to do – teach'. Summers (1981), reporting a student data-base system, notes the time saving, the ease of sorting, updating and presenting. 'Software that can save an entire man-year' is a claim made for a system developed by the Polytechnic of North London and the London borough of Enfield, and adds weight to this argument.

The desirability of computer-based administration in terms of improved efficiency is justified not only in saving work and time, hence the emancipation of teachers from clerking to teaching, but also in terms of improved information provision that can assist in teaching and decision formulation. The point made by Dooley and others should not be overlooked in this euphoria, however. Innovation requires a lot of work, study and revision. The development and implementation of computer-based administration is no exception, and advantages gained later will have to be paid for during the innovatory period. Giblin (1984), in an article beginning: 'Why are so many people working on artificial intelligence? Why don't they concentrate on the real thing?' he goes on to record: 'what concerns me here is not the relatively low numbers of computers which behave like humans in certain respects, it is the relatively large number of humans who behave like computers in certain respects. One example: people who earn their living doing jobs that could be done by a robot.' Or teachers who spend their time sorting information and writing lists which could be done by a computer and interfaced printer.

Desirability in terms of the content of a file needs careful consideration, as this can have profound consequences as to the use made of the stored information, and implications in terms of invasion of privacy. LAMSAC (1974) is useful reference here, as the project team spent considerable time and effort in establishing the file content and structure. The project was, however, making proposals from a local education authority viewpoint (which is understandable, as they were providing the funding for the project). As Bird (1982) comments:

> The report looks at the administrative and information needs of a local education service. . . . Despite the fact that much of the data on a 90 item pupil record must be collected in schools, the report is largely concerned with the benefits which will accrue to the Local Authority. A small section (page 41) identifies 8 ways in which there would be benefits in managing a school.

The proposed pupil record would not, I suggest, gain much support from teachers, as the advantages to the school, hence staff and pupils, are minimal, whereas the imposed work load to gather data would be considerable. As a total information system the LAMSAC ideas and proposals cannot be denied. The modular concept (Fig. 3, LAMSAC, 1974, p. 12) shows the compass and extent of the proposed system. The need for such detailed information must be questioned, however. The potential users of the gathered file (Fig. 4, LAMSAC, 1974, p. 10) are listed, and this again emphasises the comprehensive nature of the files. Again the need for such detailed information on every member of the school population must be questioned, especially as the providers of the information – the school, hence the pupils – have no control over its use or abuse. At present such information may be held in a school's file system but it is unlikely that the details will be as complete for every pupil as the LAMSAC report requires. At present the school is responsible for extracting and providing information essential to local authorities; why should this *status quo* be altered? At present the 'problem cases' are identified in schools, and appropriate reference is made to supportive external agencies; why should this

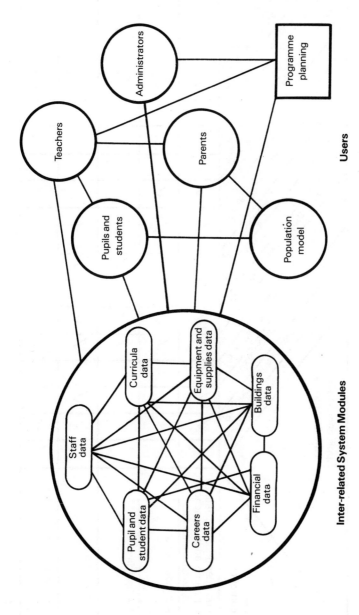

Users

Inter-related System Modules

Fig. 3

File contents — Applications using these contents

File contents	Examination entries	Secondary school selection	Awards allocation	Population forecasts	Welfare information	Youth employment	Recoupment	Pupil monitoring	Screening for special education	Pupil reports	Transport scheduling	Form 7 stats.	Attendance returns	Medical information	Health appoints.
Pupil identification data eg: name, address, school, age, sex, parents, etc.	✓	✓	✓	✓	✓	✓	✓	✓	✓	✓	✓	✓	✓		✓
Attendance data				✓	✓		✓	✓	✓			✓	✓		
Medical data				✓	✓		✓	✓					✓		✓
Welfare data		✓		✓	✓		✓	✓					✓		
Educational progress data	✓				✓		✓	✓	✓				✓		

Fig. 4

responsibility and care structure be removed? The cynical teacher may also comment that little enough use is made of the information gathered at present; why collect more? The contention here, then, is that the LAMSAC proposals go beyond the needs of the education authority whilst also failing to assist with the administrative requirements of schools. The information that would have been useful to schools was purposely excluded by the project on grounds of file size and value! Such exclusion would invalidate one of the original aims of the project, namely to eradicate the duplication of files. If the LAMSAC pupil record does not satisfy school needs, then an alternative duplicate record would have to be established.

The SCAMP (1982) project offers an alternative solution which better realises the criteria that this chapter argues for. One of the aims of the project was 'to examine the total information requirement for secondary schools taking into account SED, Regional and Divisional requirements'. The emphasis here is more appropriate, the solution of school administrative problems being the priority. From a well structured school system the needs of super-authority are more easily met. The proposed development in phase 1 of the project defines four essential aspects within the school data base:

1 The school definition file.
2 The basic pupil file.
3 The pupil curriculum file.
4 The pupil external achievements file.

These compare favourably with the components identified from the Rushby definition referred to earlier.

Both SCAMP and LAMSAC note the need for a common system to be employed within schools, if not nationally, at least within a local authority. Tomasso (1982) also reasons against 'go it alone' and, despite Green's (1979) counter that home-grown best satisfies home needs, the value of a common system is well founded. A common system does not imply a centralised system, but simply that school-based files are stored in compatible ways. This would facilitate ease of transfer of information in a common format to:

1 Another school if a pupil moves.
2 External agencies whose assistance is requested.
3 Education authorities when statistics/extracts are required.

The establishment of a common system does, however, require

initiative from a central authority. Until projects of the scale of SCAMP are launched and funded, progress will continue to occur in unrelated directions and the wheel will have to be invented in many schools.

Whilst mainframe systems have the advantage of large memory and multiple access facility, their cost and susceptibility to interference and/or corruption (be it accidental or contrived) are disadvantageous in this context. Microcomputers are 'growing', and school-based administration is within their scope. They present a lower security risk, as they are controlled by one agency – the school. Using the school micro rather than the town/county hall mainframe avoids inflaming privacy invasion arguments, as such apply equally to paper/card records as to micro-based records. Finnberg (1977) has suggested that 'the impact of computers on privacy has been exaggerated'. The opinion seems reasonable in this context, provided that the records are stored within school, on a microcomputer. Reliance is then placed upon the integrity of the user, and the situation differs little from the present practice of restricted access to the 'filing cabinet'. Security can be further enhanced by use of a menu system that would allow access only to appropriate users, perhaps by a code name or number. Provided that such restrictions apply, and that pupils and parents are aware of the records, and regular validation and updating occur, there should be few justifiable reasons for complaint.

To conclude, it has been argued that computer records should be school-based, whilst the software is designed to facilitate also supra-authority needs. A common system would be extremely advantageous but requires projects on the scale of SCAMP. Files stored should contain only appropriate information, and validation procedure should be continuous.

The final question of desirability impinges upon the structure of any system. Tomasso (1982) gives some guidelines, and these proposals are realised in the SCAMP development. The characteristics that could be reasonably expected from any proposal/developments are:

1. Common system – facilitates transfer.
2. Ease of use – to *all* users.
3. Flexibility – specialised requirements options.
4. Ease of alteration.
5. Validation structure.

6. Efficient sorting system.
7. Variable-output formats.
8. User-validation security system.

Allying these characteristics with earlier comments concerning file content provides the system outlined in Fig. 5.

Feasibility

Pupil record systems exist for both micro and mainframe systems. SCAMP (1982), Summers (1981), *Recorder* and many others give validation to the claim that computer-based school administration is possible. Commercial programs are advertised in the literature and claim to have solved many administration problems. Titles such as 'Pupil list admistration', 'Report', 'Examination entry programs' or 'Option' give a flavour of the areas catered for. The results of a 'National Administration Survey' reported by Shaw (1984) record some 40 per cent of the sample making use of microcomputers for administrative tasks. However, the survey also noted that most are 'in house' developments. Similarly Slater (1983) notes this trend and further comments: 'few have been considered for implementing elsewhere'. The conclusions of Bird (1982) emphasise the problem to be solved:

> very little external software is being used for micro-computer based administration – MCBA (only 12% of schools).

> very few schools (10%) have traced external help for MCBA.

> effort in program writing is being duplicated since many schools are beginning MCBA in isolation.

> in 50% of schools all the software is prepared by one teacher.

The need for central initiative has been discussed earlier. The present situation can be construed in terms of Havelock's (1969) 'problem-solver model'. The need existed and was identified in schools; suitable resources were sought and not found; development occured in-house. Unfortunately such strategy has led to an unsatisfactory conclusion. The need is for outside assistance, as directed in the Havelock-derived Bolam 'task consultant model'. Similarly Bolam's (1975) ideas of 'user, innovation, change agent' direct towards a consultant/external change-agent process. The

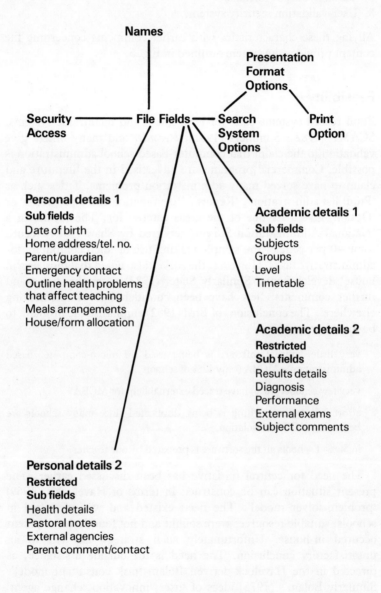

Names

Presentation Format Options

Security Access ——— **File Fields** ——— **Search System Options**   **Print Option**

Personal details 1
Sub fields
Date of birth
Home address/tel. no.
Parent/guardian
Emergency contact
Outline health problems
that affect teaching
Meals arrangements
House/form allocation

Academic details 1
Sub fields
Subjects
Groups
Level
Timetable

Academic details 2
Restricted
Sub fields
Results details
Diagnosis
Performance
External exams
Subject comments

Personal details 2
Restricted
Sub fields
Health details
Pastoral notes
External agencies
Parent comment/contact

Fig. 5

180   Teachers, computers and the classroom

establishment of such an agency, provided with appropriate funds and resources, is essential to future development if commonality and integration is hoped for. The extent of resource provision is well illustrated by SCAMP, where the project development team included a systems analyst, two computer experts, school representatives, etc. Similarly SCAMP gives an idea of the financial commitment necessary, reporting an introduction cost of £20,000 per school (albeit in mainframe access provision).

Central initiative would also help solve the hardware requirement question. Bird (1982) illustrates the breadth of contention/indecision in the field of microcomputer-based administration:

> the microcomputers in greatest use are the RML 380Z (49%) and the Commodore Pet (30·5%). [It must be remembered that the BBC micro has gained prominence since Bird's work.] In general there appears to be greater implementation on disk-based machines, but this cannot be conclusively substantiated from the data. . . . in general there appears to be greater implementation on machines with larger memories, but this cannot be conclusively substantiated from the data.

Shaw (1984) simply notes discs and printers as essential hardware. National or local developments would direct towards a particular micro with a particular minimum memory size, etc., and should ideally give assistance to establishments to obtain the hardware.

The question of staff is also essential to these considerations. Bird, noting that often only one person is responsible for the production of software – a situation that has been described as a recipe for disaster – raises the question of what happens when he or she leaves the school or the district. Such in-house developments are unlikely to be well, if at all, documented, and adaptation to future needs and demands – a point that Maddison (1982) warns against – will prove difficult. A common system, appropriately documented, would guard against such problems.

It has been reasoned that the full potential of computer-based administration will not be realised until the initiative is taken and an adequate common system developed, funded and employed. This is not, however, to deny the achievements to date, and it seems unreasonable, despite the logic of Tomasso, to argue that computer use in this field is not feasible by in-house innovation. It must certainly be admitted that progress will not be made at all, in many instances, unless such non-ideal innovation is attempted. The essential point is that the waiting game will achieve nothing.

Conclusion

It has been argued that the use of computers for storing pupil records is desirable in terms of improved efficiency. Time saved and improved availability of information, to assist both in decision-making and in teaching, are offered as justification. A pupil data base could usefully be extended to provide facilities to solve other administrative tasks, such as option grouping, timetabling, etc. Detailed discussion of the possibilities or the use of word-processors is beyond our present compass, but are essential corollary considerations.

The location of the records, centrally or within schools, was questioned, and maintenance of the *status quo* argued for, justified in terms of the 'need to know', utility and the infringement of privacy. Such considerations did not deny the needs of supra-authority, and it was emphasised that any developments must include provision for extraction and statistical analysis. Appropriate characteristics for any proposals were considered, and an outline pupil file was generated. Again this would need to be seen as part of a larger administration system – or one of a 'suite of programs', to quote the advertisers – if the full potential of the computer is to be realised. The need for a central agency to fund and develop computer-based administration was argued in terms of classical innovatory models. Such consultancy developments would solve many of the problems that have arisen as a result of the present unstructured and unrelated attempts to avoid Giblin's criticism.

Pupil record systems using computers are both desirable and feasible. Hopefully SCAMP and other enlightened groups will provide the means to a full and successful implementation.

References

Bird, P. (1982), *The Use of Low-cost Microprocessor-based Computer Systems in School Administration and Management*. London: Department of Education and Science.

Bolam, R. (1975), 'The management of educational change: towards a conceptual framework', in V. Houghton, R. McHugh, and C. Morgan (eds.), *Management in Educational Change*. Milton Keynes: Open University.

Cowie, F. (1976), 'Some experience in the use of a computer in school admistration', *Computer Education*, 22, February, pp. 11–15.

Dooley, J. (1983), 'The organisation of an efficient system', *Educational Computing*, September, p. 27.

Finnberg, D. (1977), 'Keeping personal secrets from prying eyes', *Computer Education*, 26 June.

Gallagher, T. (1982), 'The taming of Form 7', *Educational Computing*, November, p. 21.

Giblin, R. (1984), 'Citizen 2000', *Electronic Systems News*, spring, p. 10.

Green, R. (1979), 'Administration on a school microprocessor', *Computer Education*, 33, November, p. 13.

Havelock, R. (1969), *Planning for Innovation through Dissemination and Utilization of Knowledge*, Ann Arbor: Centre for Research on Utilization of Scientific Knowledge, Institute for Social Research.

Jenkins, H. and Melhuish, C. (1983), 'Teachers have better things to do', *Educational Computing*, July/August, pp. 24–6.

LAMSAC (1974), *Towards a Computer Based Education Management Information System*. London: Local Authority Management Service and Computer Committee.

Maddison, A. (1982), *Microcomputers in the Classroom*. London: Hodder & Stoughton.

Piddock, P. (1975), 'Computers in school administration: DES Form 7', *Computer Education*, 21, November, pp. 19–21.

Rushby, N. (1979), *An Introduction to Educational Computing*. London: Croom Helm.

SCAMP (1982), Scamp project – developments up to 1982, information guidelines, Glasgow: Scottish Microelectronics Development Programme.

Shaw, A. (1984), 'Nationwide administration survey', *Educational Computing*, February, p. 31.

Slater, B. (1983), 'The Computer in School Administration'. MEd thesis, University of Birmingham.

Summers, M. (1981), 'A microcomputer student data base', *Computer Education*, 37, February, pp. 34–7.

Tomasso, C. (1982), 'What if . . . and all that? – the microcomputer as a management tool', lecture, Dundee College of Education, April 1983.

Software

Assess, Sixteen-plus chemistry assessment procedure (1983), C. W. Butcher and D. Lloyd. *Recorder*, pupil data file (1983), E. Vincent.

15. So far, so good . . .

Some overall considerations

IVAN REID

In the preceding chapters we have viewed some of the ways in which teachers are using microcomputers in the classroom and some of the considerations and consequences. Perhaps more is revealed of promise than achievement, and this is hardly surprising, given that we are at the stage of introduction rather than development. In this chapter our attention is drawn to the issues raised by this book, to review the state of play and explore something of the potential and the future.

An early recognition must be that there is little room for scepticism over the growing importance of computers in education. Such scepticism arises in some teachers who, like the writer, have witnessed as pupil or teacher the supposed revolutions of radio, television, teaching machine and language laboratory. All these were heralded as replacing teachers and changing the face of education and classrooms. In the event their effects have been minimal, other than in particular circumstances and at the hands of well endowed enthusiasts. So some teachers and many others may well be inclined to sit back and wait for this latest 'fad' to either go away or become the province of a newly emerging specialist. Such attitudes are ill founded, for three principal reasons. First, the growing use of and reliance on computers and information technology in society at large is assured and unparalleled. Second, and as a consequence of the first, the insistence of government (through the DoI initiative and the setting up of MEP) and society on the inclusion of the use of computers in schools is unprecedented. Third, the potential of the present generation of computers overshadows that of any other educationally associated or useful invention, while the prospect of further advance is near to hand.

There is an abiding concern which, while not featured in this book, is attendent upon all major curricular innovation and may well be particularly pertinent in the case of computers. This is the potential for control over what goes on in classrooms, which can take a variety of forms. Computers have been placed in our classrooms by governmental edict, though, as yet, their use has not been prescribed. However, it is relatively easy to see computers as 'threatening' to classroom actors and activity. Traditionally classrooms have been labour-intensive, and technology either peripheral or used as an adjunct of the teacher. In other such fields computers are having a dramatic effect. In offices the introduction of word-processors has led to levels of efficiency that have dispensed with jobs and radically changed social institutions. The potential of computer-based curriculum management has yet to be realised and appreciated. In Utah, according to Gray (1983), it led to a restructuring of teachers' work, with a lessening of pupil–teacher interaction and an increase in testing, administration and teacher-proof learning resources developed centrally by the school authority.

Computers are obviously far more potent a force than the mandatory use of a syllabus, prescribed textbook or learning resource. Not only is the clear technological possibility of curriculum conformity almost upon us, but it will be wrapped in the persuasive values of modernity and necessity. To challenge it will be to run the risk of seeming anti-technological, Luddite even. Indeed, the use of computers in the classroom may have even more fundamental and unquestioned effects, as Young (1984) has suggested:

> To refer to the instructions one gives to a computer as a language, and to assume that it will not be long before computers can be given instructions in ordinary English, is to take over a concept of language as a set of rules or procedures and vocabulary, rather than a set of meanings embedded in history and particular social contexts. The problem that has yet to be examined is that the development of an uncritical competence in communication with computers may actually inhibit students from becoming articulate in human communication. The difference being that the meanings given to instructions by a computer will always have been preprogrammed. They will not, as in human communication, be in part the spontaneous outcome of particular situations. This is not an argument against the teaching of programming but unless the very notion of a computer language is submitted to critical analysis, the 'hidden curriculum' of computer studies is likely to remain unexamined.' [p. 208]

A similar perspective to that for the teachers can be developed for pupils. Computers are capable of recording pupils' success, or otherwise, together with indications of the difficulties, effort and time involved – which are at present largely hidden from the teacher. Learning, like teaching, might become much more clearly defined, public and controlled. Pupil and teacher accountability could be precise and continually monitored. This, however, is speculative, though the possibilities need to be kept in mind and taken into account by all those involved in schooling and education. It may be that the nature and vagaries of the British system of education, well illustrated in this book, may save schooling from such fundamental change as is apparently endemic in computer technology. Time will tell.

In any case, as we have seen more than once in the preceding chapters, the use of computers in schools appears as yet, for a variety of reasons, to be quite severely limited. The fundamental and probably long-lasting problem here is the availability of sufficient hardware to enable meaningful 'hands on' experience for the school population. If the schools studied in chapter 4 are typical (and there is no particular reason to believe that they are not) then only 50 per cent of school-leavers have any meaningful interaction with computers and perhaps only 10 per cent of them are adequately prepared for 'living with computers'. The variation in the quantity of hardware in schools and the organisation of its use raise a series of potentially major problems. If the number of computers in a school is dependent upon, or affected by, the policy and/or generosity of local authority, parents and supporters, then it is easy to predict that provision will be along the well established and traditional lines of differentiation of educational provision in Britian. 'Public' and middle-class schools will add to the present advantage of their attenders over those in LEA and working-class schools. In the present social, political and economic climate there would appear to be little hope of avoiding this situation, which is already apparent. It must then be recognised that the provision of a computer in each school is not an egalitarian policy, but simply a pump-priming move. There are likely to be some tricky decisions over the use of resources, since both hardware and software are expensive by comparison with the normal fare of schools. The diversion of limited resources into computers, while enhancing learning there, is bound to detract from more basic and essential activities. The position will be exacerbated if the use of computers in upper schools is limited to, or directed towards, examinations. Achievement in 'computer studies' could quickly become a further wedge of advantage between the achieving and the non-achieving child, both in school and, more important, in occupational opportunity. We may well be about to witness the latest variation on the classical theme of the 'haves' and 'have nots'.

Of course, the concerns of the contributors to this volume, and possibly most of its readers, are of a different order. The former provide insights into the coping strategies of teachers in classrooms with a computer. These provide reflections into and out of more general considerations. Overall the book is very much a view of pioneering work with the unfamiliar and untried – from the technical to the social; from how to operate a machine, through exploring the potential of software and learning how CAL 'fits' into school and classrooms, to evaluating its outcomes. Most of the work is limited, on-going and question-raising, and it may well be that the establishment of 'good practice' (which others may follow with confidence) is a long way off. However professionally and personally disconcerting interim resolutions may be to teachers, they appear as a growing aspect of their workaday lives. It seems likely that the development of the educational use of computers in a random way – or at least in a way that depends upon a host of unpredictable variables, not least of which is the enthusiasm of individual teachers and schools – will continue to characterise at least the next decade. Hence our consideration turns now to some of the issues and tensions raised by and between the preceding chapters.

Functional and structural questions

Chapter 2 posed two direct questions, a functional one – what can the computer do to assist learning? – and a structural one – does the computer give us grounds for changing our conceptions (and, indeed, subsequent practices) of teaching and learning? In effect all the chapters tackle these questions, though the clarity with which they address them separately varies. It is easy to agree with Bradshaw that our answers must remain provisional, since we have as yet only begun to explore a potential in a rather shallow way, and that the impact of the computer will be much greater than that of the printing press, significant though that was. There is an interesting source of tension between his conclusion that CAL will free the teacher from being 'foreman to the drudgery of fact-gathering and skill practice', releasing time for the guidance of the young in finding meanings, purposes and values, and the emphasis of other chapters. For example, several reject the idea of the computer as a teaching machine, to be used only, or mainly, for drill and skill activities. Indeed, it is chapter 3's claim that there are more exciting and worthwhile things to do, particularly the involvement and heightening of cognitive demand. Such uses would demand that teachers view thinking as more central than facts or final and correct answers – a difficult shift in the context of schools which appear to assume that thinking develops almost automatically though the mastery of factual learning and exercise. While the effectiveness of computers in the direction of thinking may as yet be limited by an inability to reflect (to differentiate between answers in the right direction and usefully redundant thinking as opposed to right and wrong), this may be only a question of time. Meanwhile it appears that teachers are predominantly exploring functional aspects of computers and that incidentally raised structural factors are dealt with *ad hoc*.

This response is well illustrated by most chapters in the book, though with some marked and interesting variations. Overall, and not surprisingly, the picture is clearly one in which the computer is used as an aid, rather than a replacement for, or alternative to, the teacher. The SCAN analysis in chapter 7 shows that, by comparison with both theory and practical ones, CAL lessons induce (or result in) more individual/group work, more freedom for the teacher to discuss rather than instruct, greater depth of demand and open questioning, more task oriented pupil–pupil discussion, more vocalisation and development and testing of hypotheses. These would generally be viewed as 'improvements' in the light of our knowledge of the process of learning, and have structural as well as functional implications. It is clear that similar effects are witnessed in the use of simulations and adventure games with primary school children in chapter 8, and in the use of word-processing functions as in chapter 13. Elsewhere computers are observed being used as more direct aids to teaching. For physics teachers they can be electronic blackboards, calculators with graphical displays, and data loggers (measuring, storing, processing and displaying measurements), as in chapter 9. Geography teachers in chapter 12 used the computer to reinforce learning or to provide for revision at the end of teaching sequences, in strongly teacher-directed lessons. As Wiegand notes, however, this may have been affected by their normal teaching style, shortage of time, the novelty of being observed and the nature of the programs used. The use of a computer data base in history lessons appears to have enhanced the children's questioning compared with traditional lessons and it is interesting to note the number of questions the computer could not answer (chapter 11).

One of the most dramatic effects of computer use for teachers is likely to lie in the yet relatively underdeveloped field of word-processors. Although the observations in chapter 13 suggest that initially children used the machines mainly for correcting mistakes rather than editing and composing, the potential is considerable. How will teachers react to the presentation of machine-printed, precisely laid out, edited and machine-spelling-checked work from pupils? Something of the challenge in the possible passing of writing skills can be gleaned from the experiences of coping with classes who 'at the touch of a button' can compute a square root to x decimal places. In written work the increments for pupils in terms of pleasure and pride in presentation appear obvious and appealing, while the learning potential of such opportunities are considerable and might well benefit all those using the written word—including teachers.

As chapter 6 reminds us, the decision to use a computer in the classroom leads to the evaluation of particular programs. The teachers who helped devise and refine the evaluatory check list in that chapter have clearly differentiated between management and educative content. One is led to believe that the latter is the foremost consideration and within that the crucial questions will typically be 'Does the approach fit in with your aims?' 'Does the content fit in with the learning objectives for your class?' 'Can the teaching or practice which the programme claims to provide be achieved more efficiently using a more traditional method?'

It is reasonable to conclude that at present the computer is just another tool in the teachers' work kit. It appears to be neutral, neither necessarily friend nor foe, helper nor usurper. The use and potential of the computer remain firmly in the teacher's professional control. Undoubtedly the pressures towards CAL will increase, and may eventually become an obligation, though to date only a small minority have taken up such opportunities as exist— as chapter 5 illustrates. There is evidence that its use does not entail conformity, even where software and purpose are in common. The traditional, individual integrity of the teacher is not, as yet, threatened.

Some overall considerations   189

Who uses computers in classrooms?

It is clear that only a minority of teachers are involved as yet, and that there are major imbalances between curricular areas and the sexes in combination, as demonstrated in chapter 5. In secondary schools, mathematics and science teachers are the predominant users and providers, in respect both to their own subjects and to computer studies itself. Elsewhere in the curriculum, and in primary schools, use appears to be related to teacher interest and ability. This raises the question as to whether such *ad hoc* development is desirable and/or whether there are any viable alternatives.

On the one hand, mathematics and science both have obvious uses for computers and CAL, were first into the field and are, therefore, the most developed (see chapters 9 and 10). On the other hand, not all teachers of those subjects even the ones entering the profession, are necessarily well equipped for, or desirous of, central involvement in computer use and service. Further, both areas are notoriously 'shortage' subjects and the deflection of staff can detract from basic teaching in the discipline. This is exemplified in chapter 10, where non-mathematics staff teach the subject lower down the school in order to release mathematics staff for computer teaching. Even within the two disciplines a serious limitation is placed on the use of computers by the lack of hardware, few departments having either their own or sufficient numbers of machines for the purposes. Further, this book has explored something of the potential for the use of computers across the whole range of curriculum and age groups. As the process gains momentum so the demands on existing hardware will be multiplied. Consequently, for some time to come there are going to be severe problems of priority in the use of computers.

Such problems seem likely to continue to be resolved within schools, perhaps mediated by LEA and government policy. The consequence will be variation, adding a further dimension to the already wide spectrum of educational opportunity and provision. How crucial computer education is to become will ultimately be measured by its reward in the occupational market. Despite previous experience of the dubious job-market value of technical as opposed to academic school achievement, the signs are that computer skills may rapidly become a condition of many forms of employment. In the primary sector any wide variation in the use of CAL is likely to pose problems for secondary schools receiving intakes from several feeder schools whose involvement may well be different in kind and extent. Arguably the problems will be even greater for the children. Again, this might be seen as simply an addition to the present considerable variation in other disciplines, but it may become more serious than that.

Computers for what?

Perhaps the most fundamental unanswered question is the use or uses to which computers should be put in schools. This book has concentrated on CAL, and there is clear tension or conflict between this use and examinable Computer Studies, particularly in a context of limited resources. CAL has the potential to enhance learning for *all* children and may particularly benefit the less able or those with special educational needs. Examination-based computer education will be of more direct benefit to the more able, who already receive a relatively high proportion of educational resources. There are pressures pulling towards the development of both these areas. History would suggest that the latter, because of its higher status and assumed direct relevance to jobs and the economy, will hold sway. A parallel problem arises in respect of staff. Should all be expected to use computers, or should their use become the developed specialism of a few, and should the level of specialism vary between the sectors of schooling?

A major issue underlying such considerations is the level of familiarity with computers that is deemed necessary for both pupils and staff (taking it for granted that computer skills and knowledge have entered the canon of education in the 1980s). It is easy to see that, predictably, the initial educational response to computers, as with most forms of new knowledge, has been classically academic. Some syllabus and teaching appears premised on the assumption that everyone needs to be an expert, capable of an understanding and appreciation that includes the ability to write programs and full knowledge of the technical and developmental aspects of computers. Such assumptions are at least questionable, in the light of the average person's knowledge of other everyday artefacts – cars, washing machines, telephones or pocket calculators. Of course, the analogy is somewhat limited, and it seems likely that if computers are to become as common as is predicted they will also become much more user-friendly. Time may well show the current educational response to be premature, since developments such as voice control, menu programmes, simplified keyboards and the like will make redundant many of the present skills for the majority of users inside and outside classrooms. Technical advances may transform the teacher use of the computer to a level similar to the self-loading projector or the video machine. Clearly there will remain a need for higher-level skill and knowledge, but only for the few, and this may be gained beyond the classroom. For the majority of pupils and teachers, if not all, only user-skills may be required.

This is speculative and hardly useful in any direct way at the present. However, it is not uncommon to see computer-based lessons in which the resulting programme is of questionable utility or marked inferiority to existing programmes. This is often achieved by pupils without the most basic of user skills, that for the QWERTY keyboard, a skill which could easily be learned at an early age and without access to a computer. Put simply, then, it would be possible to devise a systematic, developmental and incremental programme to introduce pupils (and teachers) to user skills without many of the questionable frills. Such a course might be spread through a child's school career, avoiding the development of a separate curricular identity and relieving the strain on hard-pressed hardware and personnel resources. However, it would require some central planning and provision which would run counter to existing characteristics of the British system.

Computer-assisted administration

This is an area in which a more universal appreciation of computer use might be anticipated. Chapter 14 outlined the potential for computer-based pupil record keeping and assessment recording. Word-processors are a clear boon for the writing and updating of references, the production of personalised letters, school publications and so on. Timetabling, despite early and recurrent hiccoughs in programming, may soon become a routine short undertaking rather than a term's work for a senior member of staff. In these areas the obvious spin-off in terms of time saved in recording, updating, retrieval and storage may well be transparent enough to induce even the least enthusiastic to master the necessary skills.

Constraints on the use of computers in the classroom

The contraints on developing the use of computers in classrooms are threefold – hardware, software and personnel – and appear considerable. As we have seen, teachers already involved view the limitations of the hardware available as a severe handicap, and any broadening of use would make the situation worse. It is clear that some schools are taking steps to increase their number of machines. The ability to do so varies and may lead to wide diversity of provision and access. Technological advance and an expanding choice of hardware are likely to bring a need for updating and change which will contribute further to the already complex and *laissez-faire* provision – unless, that is, there is further government or LEA initiative. At present it seems that the existing patchwork will merely strike an even bolder pattern. Only action directly related to existing provision and need could result in any increase of equality.

There are several indications in this book of what might be termed teacher resistance, or disinclination, to the use of computers. A multiplicity of factors are involved here. Innovation in education, unless enforced, or imperative, is typically far from rapid, and it may be that our view is too early for a useful judgement to be possible. The complexity of the task of teaching, especially in hard-pressed times of conflicting demands and objectives, is bound to engender in many a lack of interest, or a wait-and-see attitude, towards the new. It is easy to see that among those who have attempted to get involved some will have reacted against problems due to lack of, or competition for, hardware, together with the limitations of software. The latter are a problem even for current users. For example, in chapter 9, teachers are reported producing their own programs; many do not have the time, inclination or ability. The same source suggests that the answer lies, in the future, with both commercially produced and teacher-educator consortia, whose programs will more accurately meet classroom and learning demands identified by teachers rather than by computer experts or salespersons.

It is easy to see 'resisting' teachers' attitudes as both professional and functional. Teachers are usually open to new methods when they can perceive their utility and are provided with contexts that make their use feasible. Neither condition appears to be fulfilled in the majority of teachers' minds so far. In holding such attitudes teachers are not dissimilar to the general public. Both groups need persuading of a product's utility and so provide a direct stimulus to producers to tailor their products to consumer needs and to make information available. In general we do not ask teachers to write the textbooks they use, or to be party to their production. At the same time we do expect them to use their professional judgement about choosing and using them. In some people's minds this is precisely what should be expected of them as regards computers. It is an open question whether or not in the long run the packaged use of computers will hold sway. The machine's interactive potential – for teachers and learners alike – is obvious, though exploiting it calls for a major investment of resources and goodwill which may or may not be forthcoming.

There is a further and significant difference: the novelty of computers and the ignorance of most teachers about them. As pupils at school, few will have seen, let alone used one, and new entrants to the profession are not much different. Only thirty-one students reading for PGCE in 1983–84 took computer studies as their main course, and most of those taking it as a subsidiary were mathematics or science majors. Even of those with some education in this direction some did not wish, or had reservations about, teaching in it (see chapter 10). Such a situation clearly calls for widespread computer education for teachers, initial and in-service. Both levels are hampered by the lack of resources. It is axiomatic that such courses have in order to be effective, to be acutely user-oriented, classroom-feasible and demonstrably beneficial to teaching and learning. Given the existing range of teaching situations, variation in equipment and software, let alone objectives, there is a severe possibilty of mismatch between what might be offered and the needs of those attending courses. At secondary school level these would be appropriately catered for on a subject/level basis, while for primary and CAL-intensive schools the school itself is most likely to prove the best course unit. The latter suggestion is, of course, innovatory, since in-service education is typcially – though arguably unfortunately – seen as an individual concern or reward.

Our considerations so far bring into bold relief the very real need for research, evaluation and assessment of CAL and computer use. Teachers, as well as educational providers, need a far firmer basis than exists at present from which to make decisions, large and small, concerning the use of computers. Only more systematic, broader and deeper research is capable of providing such a basis. There are several discernible needs. The first is observation and analysis of on-going computer use in order to establish 'good practice' that might be copied or modified by other teachers in similar situations. The contents of this book illustrate some examples of such work. The second is in a way more fundamental and problematic, and is associated with evaluating the effectiveness of CAL both in terms of the types and quality of learning and thinking that it can invoke and in terms of its comparison with other teaching-learning methods, including the assessment in terms of the expenditure of resources.

Finally, if the major objective of using computers in the classroom is the familiarisation of pupils with computer life and work skills, then we need to explore the best way of achieving it for the majority. Among the alternatives are computer awareness courses, identifiable and/or examinable computer curriculum components, or more generalised introductions to the field within central disciplines of the curriculum made possible by the use of CAL. Before it can be achieved, it is clear, the vital first step is teacher familiarisation with computers. Hence there is a great need for increased publicity and, more important, for demonstration, discussion and involvement in order to disseminate the growing body of expertise, experience and potential in the field. It is to be hoped that the contents of this book have played some small part in what promises to be a long, involved but exciting saga.

References
Gray, L. (1983), 'Teachers' unions and the impact of computer-based technologies', in J. Megarry, D. R. F. Walker, S. Nisbet and E. Hoyle, *World Yearbook of Education, 1982/3, Computers and Education.*

Young, M. F. D. (1984), 'Information technology and the sociology of education: some preliminary thoughts', *British Journal of Sociology of Education* 5(2), pp. 205–10.

Notes on the contributors

P. M. Bradshaw is Senior Lecturer in Curriculum Studies in the Department of Education and Teaching Studies at North Staffordshire Polytechnic. He taught English in a grammar school and has a long-term interest in educational technology in curriculum design and development. He is currently working on the use of computer games in the teaching of economics.

Christopher W. Butcher is Head of Chemistry at Arrow Vale High School, a thirteen-to-eighteen comprehensive, in Redditch. He has interests in the application of CAL to chemistry and the use of computers for individualised schemes and for management and record systems.

Bob Campbell is Lecturer in the Department of Education at the University of York. After higher-degree work in biology and computer science he trained as a teacher and taught in a number of comprehensive schools. He provides courses and support for those wishing to use computers and information technology in schools, and is involved in computer-related research and development.

John L. Chatterton is Senior Lecturer in the Department of Education at Sheffield City Polytechnic. He has taught chemistry and science in secondary schools. He held a three-year research fellowship funded by British Petroleum, at Sheffield Polytechnic, into the development and evaluation of computers in science classrooms. He was also employed on the Computers in the Curriculum project at the University of London.

Richard Ennals is Research Manager of the Fifth Generation Computing Research Group at Imperial College of Science and Technology, University of London. He has taught history in schools in the UK and Nigeria and held visiting lectureships in computing in France and the USA. For four years he ran the project Logic as a Computer Language for Children supported by SERC and the Nuffield Foundation. He has published a number of articles and contributions to the field, including the books *Beginning micro-Prolog* (second edition, 1984) Ellis Horwood, and *History, Computers and Logical Thinking* (Ellis Horwood, 1983).

T. A. Ewen is Computing Co-ordinator at the Manor House School, Surrey.

Stephen Moss is Senior Lecturer at the Charlotte Mason College of Education, Ambleside. He was head teacher of a first school and has teaching experience across the primary school range. He is working with Professor M. Clark on a multi-media pack, *Micros and Language Development*, for use in initial and in-service teacher education.

P. Opacic is employed in Management Information Services at Vauxhall Motors.

David G. Reay is Senior Lecturer in the School of Education Studies at Newcastle upon Tyne Polytechnic. He taught for eleven years in primary schools before being employed as a research worker in a British and an American university. He has been involved in the design, production and evaluation of educational software, teacher education and research into the use of computers with young children. He has published articles in these and associated areas.

Ivan Reid is Senior Lecturer in the School of Education at the University of Leeds. He taught mathematics and history before entering teacher education. He has published a number of articles and contributions to the field of the sociology of education, including the books *Sociological Perspectives on School and Education* (Open Books, 1978) and *Social Class Differences in Britain* (second edition, Grant McIntyre, 1981).

A. Roberts is Lecturer in the School of Industrial Technology at the University of Bradford. His previous employment included teaching chemistry in secondary schools and working as a section leader in research and development in the iron and steel industry.

James Rushton is Dean of Education at the University of Ulster. He has taught in primary school and was a deputy headmaster before entering teacher education. He held the posts of Head of the Department of Education at C. F. Mott College and Deputy Director of the School of Education at the University of Manchester. He is co-editor of *The Teacher in a Changing Society, Education and Deprivation* and *Education for the Profession*, all published by Manchester University Press.

Neil Straker is Lecturer in the School of Education at the University of Newcastle upon Tyne. He has been Head of Mathematics and Co-ordinating Head of Study in comprehensive schools. He is currently conducting research into the causes and effects of the shortage of mathematics teachers in secondary schools.

Digby G. Swift is Senior Lecturer in the Department of Education at Huddersfield Polytechnic. He has taught physics in secondary schools in the UK and East Africa and was Head of the Physics Department and Appropriate Technology Centre of Kenyatta University College. He was visiting scholar at the Centre for Studies in Science Education at the

University of Leeds, where he surveyed the use of computers in school physics departments. At present he is producing a science-oriented 'coal mining' computer programme for the MEP and involved in a wide range of initial and in-service computer courses for teachers.

Jean D. M. Underwood is Senior Lecturer and Warden of the Computer Centre at the Derbyshire College of Higher Education. She has taught geography in several secondary schools and developed an interest in data processing and simulations in that discipline. Her current interest is the role of the classroom computer in the development of children's thinking.

Patrick Wiegand is Lecturer in the School of Education at the University of Leeds. He was a classroom teacher in both primary and secondary schools for eleven years. He has wide experience of the use of microcomputers in geography teaching and is currently interested in the classroom use of data bases.

Index

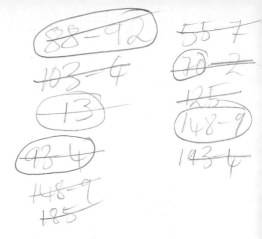